An introduc

The
Creation/Evolution
CONFUSION

H H Osborn

Apologia Publications

ISBN 978-1-901566-11-6

By the same author:

God and the antelope in the bush
The hidden key to the God-scenario
The greatest story ever told
Revival - God's spotlight

Apologia Publications

P.O. Box 3005
Eastbourne   East Sussex
UK

Contents

Unless otherwise stated, all quotations from the
Bible are from the New International Version

Introduction

The 'theory of evolution' is considered by many to be the most revolutionary contribution to science of the last two centuries. Its implications pervade the science domain and challenge basic principles in religion, philosophy, education and politics. The technical arguments are often far beyond the grasp of non-specialists.

For the Christian, the 'theory of evolution' questions the foundations of the Christian faith. This is particularly the case when there is a confrontation between what 'the Bible says' and what 'science says'. Often a contradiction is assumed without investigating what the Bible and science really say.

English is arguably the most powerful language in the world, not only because it is widely used in politics and commerce, but because its versatility makes it adaptable to all branches of science. It is used in such widely differing cultural and academic situations that, at times, each appears to have its own version of the language.

The result is that it is not infrequent for one word to have several meanings. Problems arise when the same words are used by two sides of a discussion with different meanings attributed to them. The creation/evolution debate is a good example of a situation where the communication of ideas is seriously impaired by the lack of a common understanding of words and the ideas they convey.,

The author is a mathematician whose field has been that of teaching the subject at the secondary school and university levels and of training graduate secondary school teachers. In all these fields, the requirements of the precise definition of terms, rigour of argument, criteria for judging conclusions reached and the limits of proof and demonstration are paramount. Where these are missing or not pursued adequately there is — *confusion*.

In this brief resumé of the creationist's stance, only an outline of the issues is possible. For the sake of brevity, relatively few illustrative examples are offered. Supporting literature is available.

There is also confusion between Christians in their understanding of biblical creation relative to the pronouncements of science. Such confusion sometimes makes it difficult to know what they mean by what they say and where they stand on conflicting issues.

The aim here is to clarify the terms used and hence the conclusions drawn from them rather than to pursue in depth the claims to which the terms refer. This in order to enable an intelligent understanding, if not dialogue, between those with differing views.

To differ is understandable.

Not to understand, or misunderstand the differences, is to risk *confusion*.

Chapter 1

The two stories:
Creation and Evolution
The two sources of information
The Bible and Science

The Creation story:
God created the universe from nothing. Using the created inorganic elements of the universe, He created every living organism—plant and animal, according to their 'kinds'—species between which there is cross-fertilization. Finally He created man—male and female. He did all this in six days. About 1500 years after creation, God destroyed all but eight people and all air-breathing life except a selected few who were protected in a giant ship. The destruction was brought about by a combination of a great flood and earth upheavals which raised mountains and laid down the rock and sedimentary strata that exist now.

The Evolution story:
From a spontaneous event millions of years ago, there developed a progressive evolution of all matter, subject only to natural forces obeying natural laws, to culminate in the universe as it exists now. At some point in the remote past, complex molecules of existing elements were transformed into simple living cells. From these there evolved, over long periods of time, all the forms of life that exist on planet earth today. At the same time, volcanic action and sedimentation in oceans laid down the rock and other geological strata which exist now.

Sources of knowledge: the Bible

Christians claim that the Bible is the account given by the supreme Creator-God of how the universe and people came into being, what is their purpose, what is the part they play in that purpose and what is going to happen to them in the future.

Sources of knowledge: science

Science is the investigation into the nature and behaviour of the universe and of people. It is based on observations of the components of the universe and of investigation into the way they function. Given these observations, theories are proposed as to how the components are as they are, and what are the laws or principles which govern their observed behaviour. The process of observation, formulation of theories and verification, leads to the confirmation or otherwise of the theories. Unconfirmed theories provide fields for further investigation. Confirmation establishes *assured findings of science.*

The relationship of the two sources of information:

For the Christian, the Bible records what the Creator of the universe wants people to know about His universe and about the people He has created.

Science records the findings of scientists about the nature and functioning of the universe. Science operates only in the natural world and its findings relate only to that world.

The creationist argues that, as the universe is God's creation, and science is the study of the universe, it follows logically, that

(a) science will confirm the biblical record and

(b) there is nothing in the assured findings of science which will not be in harmony with a true interpretation of Bible statements.

Differences between the two stories:

Creation	Evolution
▼	▼

Cause of beginning:

Creation	Evolution
God	Natural forces

When beginning happened:

Creation	Evolution
About 6000 years ago.	Billions of years ago.

How species of life appeared:

Creation	Evolution
God created every life-form 'after its kind'.	All life-forms evolved from the simple to the more complex.

The time life-forms took to appear

Creation	Evolution
Six days	Millions of years

When sedimentary layers and fossils formed

Creation	Evolution
Following the Great Flood	In the course of millions of years

What happens to people after death

Creation	Evolution
Heaven or hell	Annihilation

The names given to the two explanations

Creation	Evolution
The 'young earth'	The 'old earth'

A glance at the above differences will give an idea of the great gulf there is between the two explanations of the origins of the universe and of the life-forms in it.

The first most important difference between these two explanations is that *creation* requires a supernatural power while *evolution* does not. The second lies in the sources: the 'Bible plus science' *and* 'science alone'.

Specific issues which emerge from the differencies:

(a) If God is the cause of creation, creationists should be able to show that the universe and life-forms could not have appeared without supernatural intervention. If there can be no supernatural intervention, then science should be able to show that the universe and life-forms appeared without any supernatural intervention.

(b) If this is, as creationists claim, a 'young earth', and not an 'old earth' as evolutionists claim, then science should be able to provide evidence of its great age and creationists should be able to show that it could be 'young'—about 6000 years as opposed to many millions of years.

(c) If God created all life-forms after their 'kinds'—cross-breeding species, and not by an evolutionary process, then creationists should be able to show that those 'kinds' could not have been produced by a process of evolution. If all life-forms appeared by an evolutionary process, then science should be able to show that this is possible,

The grounds for confusion:

That there is conflict between the proponents of the creationist and evolutionist positions and between the claimed validity of their sources—the Bible and science, is undoubted. It would seem to be a not very difficult matter for those holding these different views to discuss them in a calm search for the truth. That, sadly is not the case.

The fact is that, the holders of the two points of view are often driven by strong motives—religious or secular.

Strong motives, hidden agendas and narrow perspectives can obscure objective thinking and cloud judgement, hence bring *confusion*.

A first step in avoiding confusion is to clarify terms so that both sides can understand what each other is saying, even if they do not agree.

Chapter 2

Clarification -
Explanatory & Hypothetical Theories
Environments

The 'theory of evolution' is the common name given to the scientific explanation of the origin of all forms of life on this planet in terms of a process of change and development from a lower or simpler form of life to a higher or more complex form.

To evolve from a life-form A to another life-form B implies a process which changes A into B. The explanation of that process is called the *'theory of evolution* from A to B'.

It is at this point that the first grounds for confusion arise. The meaning of the word 'theory' depends on the nature of the process being described. The theory can be either *explanatory* or *hypothetical*.

(a) Explanatory theory.

To illustrate the *explanatory* use of the term 'theory', imagine that I am holding in my hand a mobile phone. From it I can hear a sound reproduction of the voice of a person, possibly a long distance away, speaking into a similar phone to mine. There is nothing mysterious about that experience. It is repeated millions of times every day.

Should you be an inquiring onlooker who is ignorant of the working of the mobile phone, you might ask me to explain how I hear from that little box the reproduction of a voice spoken a long distance away. Assuming that you know enough about sound, electricity and radio waves, I would explain to you the *theory of the mobile phone*. That is, I would give you an account of the process which is quite evidently going on in terms which you would understand.

The word *theory* is, in this instance, used to describe or explain a process about which there is no doubt at all.

The *theory of the mobile phone* is an *explanatory theory*.

(b) Hypothetical theory

To illustrate the second use of the word *theory*, imagine that you board a bus and find a mobile phone on your seat. Of one thing you can be sure; that phone belongs to someone, but who? And how did it come to be there? Who would leave a mobile phone unattended on a bus seat ?

You would then formulate some theories as to how that situation came about and work out some ways of returning the phone to its owner.

One theory could be that the owner was an absent minded old person who, on getting off the bus, had forgotten to replace it in his pocket or in her handbag.

Another theory could be that someone who was using the phone had been taken ill and had forgotten or been unable to take it.

A further theory could be that a thief had stolen the phone, had seen a policeman and had got off the bus hurriedly leaving the phone on the seat.

All these theories are *imagined,* however reasonable they were. The fact that the phone was left on the seat is certain enough but the process of how it got there is not known. In order to resolve the situation, theories are formed and followed up to discover what evidence there might be available, such as whether or not the bus driver had seen someone sitting in that seat.

An imagined possibility is not an imaginary one, as in a fairy story. Such an imagined possibility is called a *hypothetical* theory—one which is proposed as a reasonable explanation for a situation or process which is not known.

The imagined possible explanation of *how the mobile phone came to be on a bus seat* is a *hypothetical theory.*

The distinguishing factor.

A 'theory' is *explanatory* or *hypothetical* depending on whether or not the situation or process which the theory describes is an established, assured finding of science of which there is no doubt.

Formulating theories of possible explanations is one of the most important ways that science uses to direct investigation into situations for which the causes are unknown. There are many instances in science where such theories have led to investigation and confirmation. When the true explanation has been discovered, the theory ceases to be a *hypothetical* one and becomes an *explanatory* one—the explanation of an assured and established finding of science.

It is an established, assured finding of science that objects are attracted to each other by a gravitational force. The 'theory of gravity' is an *explanatory* theory of the *behaviour* of gravity.

The nature of the force of gravity itself is not an established, assured finding of science. There are *hypothetical* theories which have yet to become established and assured. The terms 'established' and 'assured' refer to the nature of the evidence which distinguishes *explanatory* from *hypothetical* theories. It follows that when the word 'theory' is used without a clear understanding of whether it is *explanatory* or *hypothetical,* there is confusion.

The environments of theories

The environment of an event refers to the conditions in which that event occurs and implies limitations. The conditions of the environment determine the behaviour of a bird, an animal, or a fish. They swim, walk or fly depending on their environment—sea, land or air.

Here, for the sake of simplicity and for ease of understanding for those unfamiliar with scientific terminology, the 'environment' of an activity is taken to mean the circumstances, requirements and limits of the situation or activity. The nearest scientific terms are a 'closed system', a 'model' or a 'paradigm'.

The *theory of* an action depends on the environment in which that action takes place.

The *theory of flight* through the air for birds will be meaningless to explain the *theory of running* over the ground for animals or the *theory of swimming* through water for fish.

It is clearly important to understand the meaning of the words used relative to the environment to which they refer. To use the word 'resistance' in a discussion on the movement of fish and bird life without specifying the environment in which that movement takes place, and hence the nature of the resistance—water or air, is to lead to confusion in the communication of ideas and inevitably in the conclusions reached.

An illustration:

As the author is a mathematician, an illustration is taken from that discipline:

(a) The Euclidean geometry environment.

An example with which many who studied mathematics at school will be familiar is Euclidean geometry. In the Euclidean geometry environment, space is three-dimensional: height, width and depth are at right-angles to each other. Straight lines, curves and angles, space—area, volume, squares, circles and triangles, are all clearly defined in that environment. A straight line is the shortest distance between two points. The sum of the interior angles of a triangle is 180 degrees. Five axioms form the basis of the environment of which the fifth is: A straight line drawn through a point not on a given straight line and parallel to it will not meet or intersect the given line.

In this environment, it is possible to define situations, work logically from them and arrive at proofs. It is a satisfying experience to write QED (quod erat demonstrandum) on the bottom line of the proof of a theorem in the Euclidean environment.

(b) The spherical geometry environment.

I came to be involved in the spherical geometry environment when I was a navigator in the RAF during World War 2. I could not navigate a plane by using Euclidean geometry because the surface I was navigating over was not Euclidean but spherical. The earth is a sphere, or more accurately, an oblate spheroid. Consequently, to fly in a fixed direction was not flying along a straight line, but along a segment of a circle. Straight lines do not exist in spherical geometrical. A Euclidean geometry triangle of three straight sides is not the same as a spherical geometry triangle made up of three segments of circles. In the spherical geometry environment the interior angles of a triangle do not add up two right-angles. The term 'triangle' is, in fact, defined differently in the two environments.

It is obvious from this illustration that if two people— one working in the Euclidean geometry environment and the other in the spherical geometry environment—use the same words but with meanings appropriate to their environment, there would be confusion unless the environment is clearly understood.

For a plane to fly in a straight line from London to Edinburgh is impossible for someone working in a Euclidean geometry environment, but to fly in a fixed direction would make sense to the navigator working in the spherical geometry environment.

If a spherical geometer were to say to another spherical geometer "You go north and I will go south and we will meet in a month's time," both would understand exactly what was meant. For a Euclidean geometer to say the same thing to another Euclidean geometer, would be to talk nonsense. They would never meet. Confusion is caused when those working in two different environments attribute the same words with different meanings.

For many centuries, the Fifth Axiom of Euclidean geometry was taken to be self-evident. It was not until the 19th century that it was proved by Gauss to be true only in Euclidean geometry and not in any other geometries, including spherical geometry. The interesting deduction from this finding was that the Fifth Axiom was, in fact, not an axiom but a defining factor in determining the nature of the environment in question. If, in a geometrical environment, the Fifth Axiom is true, the geometry environment is Euclidean.

If not, not.

The two world environments.

Since the dawn of historical records, it has been recognized that, not only is there a world of physical objects and forces, but there are things happening which cannot be explained in simple physical terms. There is a physical or material world and there is a non-physical and non-material world.

Many phenomena which were not understood in the natural world many centuries ago, and were attributed to supernatural forces, have since been shown to be wholly natural. Lightning, earthquakes, diseases are examples of the many ways in which science has demonstrated natural causes to what were at one time considered to be unnatural events.

The scientific revolution not only gave natural explanations to much natural phenomena, but it gave rise to the conviction by some that the scientific environment was the only one and that everything that was not 'natural' was a figment of the imagination — it did not exist. The problem with this conclusion is that people are conscious of a great number of ideas, situations and processes which cannot be explained in scientifically detectable ways. Probably the most complex unknown process is the way the mind thinks.

Whether they are recognized or not, in practice there are two environments in which we all think, work out what to do and act.

(a) The 'natural' or science environment.

In this environment, everything that exists can be detected, directly or indirectly, by the senses—touch, sight, hearing, taste and smell. As already pointed out, radio waves and gravity are examples of indirect detection by the senses. They cannot be detected directly by the senses but mechanisms exist which indicate their existence to the senses.

A basic principle in this environment is that no entity or force exists for which there is no demonstrable verifiable evidence of a scientific nature. The whole purpose of science is to discover and use the components and forces of the natural world. It was summed up by Francis Bacon in the 17th century: "Nature, to be commanded, must be obeyed." This implies that there is a natural force responsible for everything that happens. Equally, to make anything happen it is necessary to know the forces causing the happening.

A person working in a 'natural' environment can understand ideas which are not natural but cannot accept that they exist as real objects or situations.

In the 'natural' environment, 'God' is an idea because He cannot be detected by the senses. Those working in the 'natural' environment can understand the idea of 'God' as an invisible force, but the absence of any scientifically verifiable evidence means that, in the 'natural' environment, He does not exist.

As 'colour' is non-existent in the environment of a totally blind person, and 'sound' in the environment of a wholly deaf person, so 'God' is, by definition, non-existent in the 'natural' environment of the secular atheist.

For a creationist to claim God's intervention in the origins of the universe or of life-forms, is, for the atheist, to talk nonsense. It is like discussing colour with a blind person, sound with a deaf person or a 'straight line' with a spherical geometer .

(b) The 'natural plus extra-natural' environment.

The 'natural plus extra-natural' environment includes all that is in the 'natural environment' together with all other situations or activities which are not detectable, directly or indirectly, by the senses.

It is a self-evident fact—for which there is overwhelming evidence in the world, that people are subject to influences which are not detectable, directly or indirectly, by the senses. Such influences include superstition, the occult, religion, emotions stirred by music, beauty, the elevated or tragic state of other people and even by people's own imagination.

Some of these 'extra-natural' phenomena have been the objects of research to discover evidence for their existence. An example of this is extra-sensory perception. If such 'extra-natural' phenomena are investigated and found to be detectable by the senses, they become assured findings of science and are incorporated into the 'natural' environment. Until then they are rejected by science and treated as non-existent.

The word 'phenomenon' is used here in its precise sense—that which is observed. The rising and setting of the sun is a daily phenomenon. That is what is observed. Everyone knows, however, that the phenomenon is produced by the earth's rotation about its axis. It is that movement which is scientifically verifiable.

The 'natural and extra-natural' environment includes all phenomena for which there is no natural explanation but for which there is demonstrable evidence — religion, the occult, superstition and emotions such as hysteria, love and hatred.

Proof, demonstration and evidence.

The terms 'proof' and 'demonstration' require clarification. They are often confused. Creationists are among those guilty of causing some confusion.

Proof requires that the one proving a proposition and the one being convinced share the same experience and understanding of the premises or bases of the argument.

Only in the 'natural' environment can there can be this guaranteed 'shared experience and understanding'. Only in this environment can one person be sure of an exact understanding of what another means by the terms he or she uses, and share the same experience.

I can prove to you that copper is a metal because we can both share similar sense experiences of it. Although separated in distance and time we can both be sure that we are referring to the same thing. We can make the same observations by seeing, touching and physically analyzing the metal. For instance, both of us can expose a piece of copper to a flame and see the flame turn to the same colour. We can, therefore, be sure that we both mean the same thing by the words we use.

Only in this context of shared experience can one prove anything to another person.

To refer back to the geometry environments. A Euclidean geometer can prove *only* to another Euclidean geometer that, for instance, the sum of the interior angles of a triangle equals 180 degrees. Both share the same experience of lines, angles and angular measurement. He cannot do so to a spherical geometer because both do not share the same experience of lines, angles and angular measurement although both use the same words.

By contrast, I cannot prove to anyone that 'love' or 'hate' exist although their effects are as evident in people's behaviour as those of the force of gravity. Nothing outside the 'natural' environment can be proved, but a great deal can be demonstrated.

The term 'to demonstrate' has a much wider application than 'to prove'. To demonstrate the effect of an emotion, for instance, one has only to show that the observable effect is related to the emotion. That does not constitute proof. Any one working in the 'natural' or 'science environment' requires 'proof of existence' or 'proof of function'. This can then be demonstrated to be so. The search for 'proof' is recognizably one of the great challenges of the science community and it is one through which great contributions have been made to modern society.

Evidence and proof

The confusion caused by the incorrect use of the word 'proof' is made worse when the word is used instead of 'evidence'.

The records of floods in most if not all ancient historical records is not *proof* that there was a universal flood as recorded in the Bible. But that 'evidence' *demonstrates* that it could have happened.

The rightly famous book of the 19th century by William Paley is sometimes wrongly quoted as claiming to provide proofs of the existence of God. The correct title of the book is: *"Natural theology: or Evidences of the existence and attributes of the deity, collected from the appearances of nature."* William Paley produces strong evidence for 'the existence and attributes' of God drawn from observable phenomena. That evidence is not, however, proof.

It follows from this clarification of the use of words that 'proof' is never possible for the existence of any entity or of any process which is not in the 'natural' environment. However, it is possible to present evidence which demonstrates the reasonableness or otherwise of links between unknown causes and observable effects.

Confusing claims:

(a) 'Scientists deal with facts for which there is proof, while religion deals with facts for which there is no proof.' That is correct. It is true that religion deals with facts for which there is no scientific 'proof'. The confusion arises from the assumption that the claims of science are true, whether or not they are proved to be so. Scientific *hypothetical* theories are beliefs until they are proved to be assured findings. It cannot be proved that the world and all life-forms were created by a supernatural power. Nor can it be 'proved' that they came into being by any other process. However, the evolutionist provides evidence which demonstrates the possibility of the evolutionary explanation for the life-forms being the correct one. Equally, the creationist provides evidence which demonstrates that the evolutionary explanation is not possible.

The distinction lies in the nature of the evidence for or against the theory. Where the evidence amounts to proof, the theory is an *explanatory* one. Where the evidence does not amount to proof, the theory is a *hypothetical* one.

(b) Some claim to be atheists because the absence of scientifically verifiable evidence of the supernatural or extra-natural is, for them. 'proof, that there is no God. In fact, as already observed, such an assertion, like Euclid's Fifth axiom, is not self-evident, but defines the environment. The fact that a person believes that it is self-evident that 'there is no God', does not mean that there is no God, but that the person is reasoning in a 'natural' environment.

The absence of evidence for existence in the 'natural' environment is not proof of non-existence in any other environment..

(c) For the creationist, as for the evolutionist, the distinction between 'evidence' and 'proof' is important to avoid confusion. 'Evidence' for an evolutionary link may demonstrate its possibility but it is not 'proof' of that link. Equally, the lack of evidence for an evolutionary process demonstrates, but is not proof, that it did not, nor could not take place. To ignore evidence is to limit investigation. To misrepresent it is to cause confusion.

The confusion illustrated:
An example of the confusion of words.

"Today the theory of evolution is about as much open to doubt as the theory that the earth goes round the sun." [1]

In this quotation, the word 'theory' is used twice.

In its first use, the *theory of evolution,* is , for the secular atheist working in the 'natural' environment, an *explanatory theory* of a self-evident fact which is not 'open to doubt'. For the creationist, however, working in the 'natural plus extra-natural' environment, the *theory of evolution* is a *hypothetical one ,* because there is no assured scientific evidence of its truth. A *hypothetical theory* is, by definition, open to doubt.

The second use —*the theory that the earth goes round the sun,"* is a generally accepted *explanatory* theory of an established assured finding of science. For many centuries, the observed phenomena of the sun 'rising' in the morning and 'setting' in the evening made the theory that the sun rotated round a flat earth a self-evident fact. Scientific investigation proved the theory to be wrong. That *the earth goes round the sun* is an *explanatory* theory of a process for which there is overwhelming scientific evidence

To discuss the theory of evolution without specifying whether the term refers to an *explanatory* or *hypothetical theory*, or without defining the environment in which the discussion is taking place, is to lead to confusion.

Secular atheists will only discuss the theory of evolution when it is considered as an *explanatory* theory of an established, self-evident process which requires no proof, only an explanation of the level which science has reached in understanding the accepted process.

[1] Richard Dawkins   *The Selfish Gene* p.1

The creationist, on the other hand, will not accept the
theory of evolution as established, self-evident fact and will
only discuss evolution as a *hypothetical* theory which requires proof. Demonstration of its possibility is not enough.

Unless both creationist and the secular humanist atheists recognize that they are working in different environments, attempts to communicate will result in confusion.

The quotation cited earlier makes sense to the scientist
who is limited to the 'natural' environment. For the creationist, working in a 'natural plus extra-natural environment, a rewording of the quotation would read:

> *Today the hypothetical theory of evolution is about*
> *as much open to doubt as the explanatory theory that*
> *the earth goes round the sun is open to certainty.*

Confusion is assured when the different environments
in which evolutionists and creationists think and work are
not recognized, when the term 'theory' is used without reference to the environment to which it refers, and without
clarifying whether the reference is to its *explanatory* or *hypothetical* meaning.

Chapter 3

Clarification -
Species and 'cross-fertilization'
'Random mutation' and 'natural selection'

Species of animal, bird, or plant life are those which share common characteristics which distinguish them from other species. Science is very much involved in determining these characteristics, how they are produced, the way they affect the behaviour of the species, and how they are related to where the species are to be found.

An important distinction between species or groups of species lies in how they relate to each other. There are two types of relationship. Where these are not understood or defined, there is confusion.

'Cross-fertilization', (CF)
Cross-fertilization between two species is the process by which a new variation is produced. Cross-fertilizing or CF species are those between which this is possible. There are two variations of this.

(a) Natural

Natural cross-fertilization occurs when two different CF species of animals, birds or plants produce a variation with no human intervention. This natural cross-fertilization is responsible for many variations within CF species which are to be found in the wild. The distinguishing feature of natural cross-fertilization is that the mating or pollination required is entirely natural with no human intervention.

(b) Unnatural

Unnatural cross-fertilization occurs when two different CF species of animals or plants are purposely cross-fertilized by human intervention to produce a variant. This process is well-understood and practised by horticulturists and breeders of domestic animals. The great variety of pure and hybrid vegetables and flowers, pedigree and mongrel dogs, racing and working horses, is evidence of this fact. The distinguishing feature of this unnatural cross-fertilization is that pollination or mating is humanly controlled.

(2) 'Non-cross-fertilization', (NCF) .

Non-cross-fertilization, or NCF, is the name given to the relationship between species of animals or plants between which cross-fertilization is impossible. The pairing of chromosomes between different species is impossible because the male and female cells of the species have no means of uniting as happens in fertilization or in pollination. There is no means of effecting the gene transformation necessary to produce the biological differences.

The importance of the distinctions between cross-fertilizing (CF) and non-cross-fertilizing (NCF) species, and between 'natural' and 'unnatural' fertilization, lies in the confusion which occurs when the distinctions are not recognized or the terms are misused. Probably the most frequent misuse occurs, as it does frequently, when a verified process of so-called 'evolution' between two cross-fertilizing species is assumed to apply to non-cross-fertilizing species. It is not uncommon to read in scientific journals of investigated behaviour in the so-called evolutionary path from one species to another, to be used as the basis of predictions for the behaviour of other species without any reference to their CF or NCF relationships.

The process from Alsatian to Great Dane in dog species is not the same as from dog to horse, despite the similarity between Great Dane and Shetland Pony.

Natural selection

'Natural selection' is the process by which some variations of a species continue to reproduce while others are eliminated. The selecting factor is 'natural' in the sense that it can be explained by natural causes.

Imagine that you are offered a variety of nuts from which you select one that you consider good for you. That is 'unnatural' selection because an intelligence has intervened to determine the choice. Imagine further that a selection of nuts is laid out in a clearing in a tropical forest. The monkeys there only eat, say two of the variety of nuts presented. The rest are left untouched. The nuts eaten are a 'natural selection' because they are selected by the nature of the monkeys with no human intervention.

 The word 'natural selection' implies situations where the *possibilities of choice exist naturally* and where *choice is possible naturally*, without human intervention.

The precondition for 'natural selection' to take place is that there exist possibilities from which the selection can be made. The process of selection does not provide the possibilities from which the selection is made.

Mutation

Mutation is a change in the fundamental biological structure or *genome* of an animal or plant. It is this structure which is called the DNA. It is different in every species of plant or animal.

The biological structure or *genome* of a human being is different from that of an ape. For that biological structure to evolve from that of 'ape' to that of 'man' requires more than a process which produces *variations*. It requires *mutations*, that is, changes in the fundamental biological structures of the evolving organisms.

Unlike 'natural selection', mutations are not predictable, that is, they do not happen through known natural processes. Because of this, the process of mutation is often referred to as 'random mutation'. It is not known what can cause mutations naturally, that is, without any form of genetic engineering. Their claimed occurrence conforms to no known pattern nor is it the product of any known biological mechanism, hence the term 'random' is usually added to describe the claimed process of evolution between non-cross fertilizing species.

A 'best-selling' car illustration

A simple illustration of these basic terms can be drawn from the models that a car manufacturer produces. The 'best-selling' model for any given range of cars can be considered to be a product of 'natural selection' due to market demand. It is the model which sells best.

Later, the same manufacturer produces another range of cars. Again market forces, expressed in terms of sales, produces its 'best seller'. In each case, the best-selling model can be considered to be the product of 'natural selection' from the available models of that year. Leaving aside the possible effects of the manufacturer's advertising, the car with the best-selling features sells best. The selection is not made by someone who decides which is to be the 'best-seller' but by a process in which many factors influence the choice of a variety of car buyers.

It is most likely that the car manufacturer notes the selling points of the 'best seller' of the first range and incorporates them into what becomes the 'best-seller' of the next range of models. In an engineering sense, the first 'best-seller' *evolves* into the second 'best-seller' because there will probably be many structural features which are common to both.

The 'evolution' of the second 'best-seller' from the first requires alterations in the structure. In this illustration, this is produced by engineers. The first 'best-seller' *evolves* into a new range of cars from which 'natural selection' produces the second 'best-seller' 'Natural selection' leads to the choice of the model which becomes the 'best-seller' but the 'best-seller' itself is a product of changes in its structure produced by engineers.

The car manufacturer's changes in the structure of the cars are like biological 'mutations'. The choice of the 'best-seller' is like biological 'natural selection'

'Natural selection' and 'evolution'

The 'best-selling' car story illustrates 'natural selection' in biology. It is the process by which some existing variations continue to survive while others do not. Those who buy the best-selling car may, in so doing, influence the design engineers in the development of new improved cars, but they do nothing about their production.

In nature, 'natural selection' is an important way in which the variations of a species survive depending on the conditions in which they live. The process of 'natural selection' contributes nothing to the evolution of new species.

The 'theory of evolution' claims that one species of animal or plant evolved into another by a process of 'mutation within the biological structure' and 'natural selection'. The 'best-selling' car story illustrates clearly the important distinctions between the two. One model of car could not evolve into another more complex model without the intelligence of the engineers who designed it and so produce a kind of 'mutation'. The 'best-selling' model could not emerge without the 'natural selection' of the buyers.

The scientific world attributes the 'origin of species' to 'random mutation' and 'natural selection'. The two are totally different functions. The confusion arises when the terms are used to imply that 'mutation' and 'natural selection' are natural functions which work together to produce new species. This hides the fact that 'natural selection' is, as the name suggests, *natural*, and obeys known natural laws, whereas 'mutations' are *unnatural* in that their production obeys no known natural laws. It also hides the fact that 'natural selection' only operates after the products of 'mutations' appear.

Conclusions

(a) There is a clear distinction in the relationship of species between which there is cross-fertilization (CF) to produce *variations*, and species between which there is no cross-fertilization (NCF) and hence no naturally and normally occurring biological product.

The process of 'cross-fertilization' between CF related species is a well-known, well-documented and well-established, fully assured fact of science. Its patterns of development are understood, verifiable and capable of replication. The development from one species to another by cross-fertilization is correctly referred to as producing *variations* of the same basic biological structure.

However, in biological circles it is frequently referred to as an *evolution* from one species to another without specifying the nature of that evolution. A consequence of this lack of clarity is that some evolutionary processes between species are claimed to be the same, when their only similarity lies in the confusing use of the same word.

CF Evolution, or more accurately, *variation*, is very different from *NCF evolution*. Failure to distinguish between the two leads to confusion.

(b) 'Natural selection' presupposes a number of existing life-forms which are subjected to an environment which makes it difficult if not impossible for some variations to survive. Elimination and survival are part of the function of 'natural selection'.

Sometimes 'natural selection' is described as the process of 'the survival of the fittest'. This has been challenged as simply another way of saying that the fittest are those which survive. Although interesting, this discussion does not affect the main issue which is that natural circumstances favour some members of a species more than others and this leads to the elimination of those which do not survive, and the survival or 'selection' of those which do.

'Natural selection', by definition, cannot produce new species, it can only select from existing species those which survive.

(c) For an evolution from one species to another NCF species, 'mutations' are required in the fundamental biological structure of the animal or plant. The production of mutations is not a normal process governed by known laws of genetics. They are unpredictable, hence random.

This randomness is not, however, total. The biological structure in which 'random mutations' occur will, to a large extent determine what mutations are possible and which could lead to the evolution of new organisms.

It is recognized that many 'random mutations' will be needed before any biological structures emerge which are able to survive as independent organisms. Then there will be, presumably, many such organisms which will then go through the test of 'natural selection' for survival in the existing environment. It follows, therefore, that, for 'random mutations' and 'natural selection' to take place long periods of time are required.

(d) The lack of clarity in the terms used leads not only to confusion in thinking, but also to the false accusation of what others claim.

An example of this occurs when the creationist is accused of rejecting 'random mutation' and 'natural selection'. It is true that 'natural selection' is rejected by creationists when it is coupled with 'random mutations' as if they were integral parts of the same process. However, it is not rejected by creationists, and is, in fact, accepted as part of the process of the selection of *variations* of species which survive the conditions in which they live.

The creationist misunderstands the evolutionist when the former does not understand the term 'random mutation' in the same way as the evolutionist. 'Randomness' has a scientific connotation, linked with 'chaos theory', which is far removed from the concept that the ordinary person has of that term.

Creationists can sometimes give the impression that for evolutionists to put faith in 'random mutations' is for them to believe in fairy stories, or at least to believe in what most people would understand as miraculous. The level of credibility of, say a 'one in a million chance' differs considerably and affects one's understanding of 'randomness'.

To blur definitions or to assume meanings to terms which are not true is to cause confusion in communicating ideas and sometimes raise emotions unneccessarily.

Chapter 4

Clarification -
**Complexity
Intelligent design
Irreducible complexity**

The English language is very flexible but there are some limitations. If a structure is complex, we simplify it. However, if a simple structure is made more complex there is no word for that process. Where the word 'complexify' is used it will be simply to mean that a simple structure is made more complex.

Triangle 'A' is a simple shape. 'B' is a more complex shape.

A   B

To go from B to A is to simplify. To go from A to B is to make more complex — to *complexify*!

Evolution is defined as the progressive development of simple into more complex forms of life. Hence the importance of the words 'simple' and 'complex'.

The simplest forms of life are the single cell amoeba, paramecium and euglena. They are, however, far from simple. The most complex life-forms are people. The complexity of a life form is in its biological structure. Today we call that the *genome*.

The confusion in understanding the process of evolution lies in the fact that there are two distinct types of change or development which occur in the *genome*.

Natural change - 'variation'

Natural change occurs whenever the female seed of an animal or plant is fertilized by the male. The newly emerging forms of life are similar but not exactly the same as the forms which produce them. This development, sometimes called evolution but more accurately 'variation', changes the arrangement of the genome but does not make it more complex. If a series of cross-fertilizations produces a spaniel dog from a retriever, that is a kind of evolution, but the end product is still a dog.

The genome of the retriever is no more complex than that of the spaniel.

Unnatural change - 'evolution;

The second type of change is, as has already been described, one which occurs relatively rarely and is called a *mutation* in the structure of the genome. Such a change does not operate according to normal life processes but occurs randomly. It cannot be predicted. One dictionary describes this change as "a relatively permanent change in an organism's hereditary material". Such changes are not normal and are usually attributed to 'random mutations'.

The claimed evolution from one species to another of which the genome is more complex, requires more fundamental changes than those associated with the normal processes of fertilization and pollination.

Most known mutations affect the character of the genome but do not change its fundamental structure. Engineered mutations by medical scientists usually have the aim of correcting a malfunctioning gene.

The theory of evolution proposes that from many random mutations over a long period of time, the fundamental biological structure of genomes is changed to form new more complex genomes, those of new species.

More and less complex

The evolution of a genome of one level of complexity to one of a greater complexity requires two operations: the alteration of the genetic structure *and* the formation of a new energy producing mechanism to provide the extra energy needed by the more complex organism.

It is at this point that an assured finding of science is introduced. Basic to many branches of engineering are the Laws of Thermodynamics. According to these laws—the assured findings of science, neither matter nor energy can be created or destroyed. If you put a cup of coffee in a totally sealed container it will not become more or less coffee and its temperature will remain the same. There has not yet been a situation where this does not apply.

Another law states that, in a totally closed system, an object or situation cannot become more complex because no further energy is available to it, and if an object becomes less complex in a closed system, it will lose energy.

To use the cup of coffee in a sealed container illustration, provided the container remains sealed, the only change that the cup of coffee can undergo is to become cooler—it cannot become hotter because it cannot gain energy from elsewhere. For it to become cooler it must lose some energy from the system.

By this second law of thermodynamics, matter always goes from order to disorder, from more to less complex, and loses energy in the process; never the other way round. For an organic cell to become more complex, not only must its fundamental character change but it must gain energy to make and maintain the change.

'Evolution' from a life-form to one of greater complexity requires (a) that mutations change its biological structure, (b) that it acquires the required extra energy to make the change possible, and (c) that it generates the mechanism needed to maintain the increased energy.

Scientific investigation shows that these laws apply throughout the known universe.

Intelligent design

This term is used to describe situations in the natural world which cannot be explained in terms of 'undirected natural forces' and which require an intelligence to bring about. Planet earth is a good example. Its distance from the sun determines its temperature. Its angle of inclination to the sun, its rotation and movement relative to the moon ensures the seasons needed for vegetation. The oceans and atmosphere provide the rain needed for cultivation. All these and other factors make it ideal for human occupation. No other planet has yet been discovered which combines all the features needed for human life. Planet earth appears to be an example of 'intelligent design'. It shows all the signs of intelligence in its place and functioning.

The creationist's explanation is that this is one of many situations in which can be discerned the Intelligent Design of its Creator—God.

The atheist alternative is referred to as the Goldilocks principle. All who know the fairy-story will remember that Goldilocks tried the three beds and the three bowls of porridge but in each case only one was 'just right'.

Following that argument, science claims that there are billions of celestial galaxies of which that of the sun is a small one. Even if the chances of a planet with a suitable environment were a billion to one, that would still leave millions which would satisfy the Goldilocks criterion of being 'just right'. It is argued that, where an 'intelligent design' may appear to be unique, the real cause is 'natural selection'. The so-called 'intelligent design' of the earth is, therefore, a product of 'natural selection' from many existing designs and is only 'intelligent' in the sense that it meets the requirements of human life. Metaphorically speaking, Goldilocks' search for a perfect home is rewarded when, after trying many millions of possibilities, she finds planet earth to be 'just right'.

The question of 'intelligent design' is to the fore in scientific discussions because the DNA reveals many biological structures which require a high level of intelligence to understand them and appear to bear the marks of order rather than of randomness or chance. The expression 'Intelligent design' has the advantage that it allows for a scientific investigation into the nature of, for instance, the DNA, without specifying any particular intelligence as the designer. It need not, therefore, be treated as a religious subject.

Every example of biological complexity implies an order in its structure, that is, design, in order for it to function effectively. If all biological structures were simple it might be possible to explain them as 'chance arrangements'. In fact, all biological structures, even those of the simplest cells, are very complex indeed and challenge the most intelligent of scientists to decode them.

Irreducible complexity.

Another example of complexity is expressed in the term 'irreducible complexity'. A commonly quoted illustrative example of this is the mouse-trap. It is made up of six parts. However, only when *all* those parts are in place can the trap fulfil its purpose—to catch mice. If there were only five parts, the trap would be ineffective. If the six parts were put together in any but the form intended, the trap would be useless.

There are many complex biological structures or mechanisms which function effectively in their existing forms but for which there is no less complex form known or proposed which would function less effectively or at all.

The human eye is a good example. There are other forms of 'sight' or means of detection of objects which operate effectively in bats and reptiles. None of these, however, can be envisaged as part of an evolutionary process in the human body culminating in the very complex eye.

The most powerful example of irreducible complexity is the human DNA molecule which stores coded information in more highly complex form than is possible in the modern computer. Reduce or change its vast store of millions of items of information and instructions and it ceases to function effectively.

The evolutionist's answer to this problem is to insist that what seems impossible within the time limits of human investigation is possible over very long periods of time. Given millions of years, millions of random occurrences in the natural world, and millions of 'natural selections', it is very possible to envisage the emergence of the complex cells existing now. The 'Goldilox principle' operates through millions of 'random mutations' and 'natural selections' over millions of years to produce what appear to be ' intelligent design' and 'irreducible complexity'.

The confusion in discussing 'intelligent design' and 'irreducible complexity' lies in the varying degrees to which each person is prepared to see 'design' in nature to be a natural product of 'random mutations' and 'natural selection', as does the evolutionist, or as the product of some intervening intelligence, as does the creationist.

It is not difficult to see that the atheistic Goldilocks-like presuppositions favour the *natural* appearance of design, while the God-based presuppositions of the creationist favour a *supernatural* intervention.

Conclusions

(a) As already recognized, confusion is caused by the use of the term 'evolution' to indicate both the production of *variations* within CF species and the claimed evolution between NCF species. The confusion is made worse when the distinction is not made between the '*same* complexity' of *variations* within CF species and the '*different* complexities' of NCF species.

To refer to both forms by the same word: *evolution*, is to ignore not only the difference in the way they are formed but also to hide the fact that they represent different levels of complexity.

(b) The two features which distinguish the 'increased complexity' of species, as required for evolution between NCF groups, and the 'same complexity' of variations within CF groups, are (i) a fundamental change in the structure of the DNA, and (ii) the formation of new mechanisms to provide the necessary additional energy necessary to maintain the more complex cells.

To refer to the evolution of 'more complex' life-forms as the result of 'mutations' without specifying the increased requirements in terms of energy to produce and maintain the increased complexity, is to lead to confusion.

(c) Confusion in the argument for 'intelligent design' and 'irreducible complexity' lies in the individual's subjective assessment of what is possible *naturally* and what requires *intelligent* intervention.

Science recognizes that there are many millions of life-forms of varying complexity. It assumes that the transition from simple to complex forms has been achieved by wholly natural processes. This line of argument is open to serious questions. The differences in the designs of the DNA structures of any two NCF species are fundamental.

To illustrate the problem, imagine the capital letters of the English alphabet. It is not difficult to imagine that the letter I could evolve into the letters:

C , L , M , N , S , U , V , W , Z .

However, for I to evolve into

E , F , H, K, T , X ,

would require a radical change in the structure of the letters. This would be the equivalent of a 'mutation' to change the structure of, say, the single-line L into a two-line F, or for a single-line N to evolve into a two-line E , or a three-line H. As each of the letters has a meaning, it would be natural to conclude that the final form is an 'intelligent design'. This would not be the case if the final form was either ∝ ⚴ or ⊠ which are meaningless.

The important element in this arguments lies in the extent to which people put their faith in natural processes to produce complex structures.

When the nature of claimed evolved biological complex structures are clearly recognized and when the full implications of claimed greater complexity are understood there can be dialogue.

Where they are not present, there is *confusion*!

Chapter 5

Clarification:
Blind, false and reasoned faith; superstition

It is not unusual to hear creationists described as Bible-thumping fundamentalists who believe anything they think the Bible states, however absurd that may be.

It has been known for creationists to thump their Bibles while making a point, but that thumping does not mean that they insist on blind-faith, that is, that they or their hearers accept what is written there without thought and reasoning.

'Faith' is an essential component of both the creationist's and the evolutionist's arguments. Confusion arises when assumptions are made as to the nature of the faith in question. To understand, if not to eliminate this confusion, definitions are necessary.

Blind faith and superstition

Blind faith and superstition are so closely linked that they are considered together. Both are trust or faith in someone or something with no reasoned or reasonable grounds for doing so.

Blind faith was expressed in the much sung war-time song: "We'll meet again, don't know where, don't know when, but I know we'll meet again some sunny day'. In fact, war casualties suggested the reverse. Many would never meet again alive. The faith that 'we'll meet again' was 'blind faith'.

As an example of superstitious faith, in the author's experience in World War 2, some members of aircrew would not fly without carrying a particular object or item of clothing. This was 'blind faith' in the ability of an object to protect from danger. It was, at the same time, a superstitious act because there was no reasoned or reasonable explanation except that that item of clothing had been worn on every combat mission where the air-crew member had survived.

Such superstitious acts have abounded and still do so in all societies, even those with a high scientific understanding. Even in highly civilized cities it is rare to find a hotel with a 13th floor!

'Blind faith' and 'superstition' are expressions of an irrational faith in false ideas of causation. These ideas can be religious, magical, the operation of chance or merely the imagination. The common characteristic of such faith is irrationality. It is unreasoned and unreasonable.

To accuse creationists of 'blind faith' or faith in superstition, is to insist that, either they do not apply reason to their claims, or that they apply their reason to imaginary things which do not exist in the natural environment and therefore do not exist at all.

Reasoned—false and true faith.

Reasoned faith is conviction based on conclusions reached drawn from available data. An act of reasoned faith can always be supported by reasonable grounds.

Reasoned faith is not limited to trust in scientifically verifiable facts. Even an atheist trusts in the integrity of his or her doctor. Provided there is sufficient demonstrable evidence, such faith is justified. It is reasoned and reasonable.

The difference between reasoned *true* faith and reasoned *false* faith lies in the truth or otherwise of the premises of the reasoning. For instance, faith in the ship, the Titanic, as being unsinkable, was 'reasoned faith', but it proved to be false. It was reasoned false faith.

Creationists and secular atheists apply reason to their claims. Whether their reasoning is true or false depends on which of the explanations—creation or evolution—is the correct one.

The sources of the confusion

Confusion arises when the word faith is used without an understanding of the presuppositions of those who use the word. Advice such as that of Lord Salisbury: 'never trust experts', is sound or stupid depending on the context and the objects of trust. In an environment of medical care for the seriously ill, such advice is stupid and could endanger life. In an environment where political decisions are made on the advice of political experts, the advice is very commendable.

(a) Two different environments

Confusion arises when 'faith' is given one meaning in a 'natural' environment and another in a 'natural plus extra-natural' environment

This is illustrated by two quotations from 'The God Delusion" which claim that in religion:

"Faith (belief without evidence) is a virtue. The more your beliefs defy the evidence, the more virtuous you are."[1]

"More generally, ... one of the truly bad effects of religion is that it teaches us that it is a virtue to be satisfied with not understanding." [2]

These quotations make complete sense to the atheist. It is reasonable for someone living in that environment, with faith defined as 'belief without (scientific) evidence' and 'without (scientific) understanding', to accuse the creationist of exercising 'blind faith' and of making ignorance a virtue. Faith is 'blind' where there is no acceptable evidence and where the objects of faith do not exist.

The supreme act of faith of the atheist is to believe that there is no supreme being, no God. To limit one's environment to that which is detectable by the senses only is surely intellectual folly. The above quotations reflect the environment of the atheist. For those to whom it is self-evident that absence of scientific or 'natural' evidence is proof of non-existence, it will appear that faith in the, to them, non-existent God is *"to be satisfied with not understanding"*, that is, 'blind faith'. It will follow logically from this that, where such 'bind faith' is a virtue then *"the more your beliefs defy the evidence, the more virtuous you are."*

Atheists will not discuss evolution with creationists. In fact, they cannot! They rule out of the discussion anything they believe does not exist. Creationist's do not accept the narrow view that only what is scientifically verifiable exists. Hence, for the creationist, it is the atheist evolutionist who is exercising 'blind faith' — *'belief without evidence'*.

[1] Richard Dawkins *The God Delusion* p199   [2] Idem p126

(b) The nature of facts

In theory, facts are items of information which are presented as being objectively true. In practice, many items of information are presented as 'facts' which are not objectively true but are 'believed to be true'.

As illustrated earlier, for the Euclidean geometer, it is a fact that the shortest distance between two points is a straight line. For the spherical geometer, the fact is that the shortest distance between two points is the segment of a circle. Both facts are objectively true in their environment.

Many, if not most of the facts relative to the universe and the natural world are presented in the context of the 'natural environment'. It is important, therefore, to interpret the facts presented in the light of their context.

Most science text-books present the facts of the origin of the universe and of life-forms in a context which defines existence as that, and only that, which can be detected by the senses. Such facts are: the universe began with a 'Big Bang' and is billions of years old; apes are the ancestors of human beings; birds evolved from lizards; sedimentary layers were laid down over millions of years.

The truth is that all these 'facts' are not objectively true, but are 'believed to be true' by evolutionists. Science journals and teachers rarely define the facts which they present as either objectively true or what they 'believe to be true' given the context in which they are working.

A scientific 'fact' is an assured finding of science. There are, in fact, relatively few such facts. Most 'facts' depend on evidence which is not scientific or material and hence their validity must be judged by the strength or otherwise of the demonstrable evidence.

Confusion arises when the nature of a claimed fact is not defined and a false impression that the facts presented are objectively true when they are only 'believed to be true'.

Conclusions

(a) The place of faith in the creationist/evolutionist dialogue becomes confused when each side thinks in a different environment and uses the language of that environment. Where, in an environment, a situation—religious, fairy story, or superstition, is not considered to exist, then belief in that situation is considered to be 'blind faith'. To believe that the evidence of order and 'intelligent design' in the universe demonstrates the existence of God is, for the atheist, to exercise 'blind faith', for God does not exist in his environment. For the creationist, such faith is reasoned, for the existence of God is recognized in his environment by virtue of strong supporting evidence.

(b) 'Reasoned faith', as opposed to 'blind faith', is trust in situations which are not scientifically verifiable but for which there is demonstrable evidence. For the creationist, the greater the demonstrable evidence of God in the Bible, in the universe and in his own experience, the greater will be his faith—reasoned faith. The refusal of atheistc humanists to recognize the existence of anything extra- or super-natural, despite great demonstrable evidence, means that their trust in their conclusions is 'blind faith'. It is 'belief without evidence.

(c) For those not limited to the atheist environment, the nature of faith is determined by the objects or grounds of their faith. 'Faith is grounded in facts'. True! But the presentation of facts is subject to great confusion. Facts are either objectively true or 'believed to be true'. The assured findings of science are facts which are verifiable. All other 'facts' require an understanding of their context and supportive evidence.

Where the objects and grounds of faith are not recognized and understood, there is *confusion*.

Chapter 6

The Creationist's case:
The absence of contradictory evidence

It has been necessary to clarify terms in order to argue, without confusion, the real issue — the creationist's opposition to the theory of evolution?

An important question is appropriate at this point.

Why does the creationist oppose the evolutionist?

Is it not possible to be a creationist evolutionist?

The answer is a very definite No!

The evolutionist believes that the state of the universe and all forms of life, including human beings, evolved by natural processes over great periods of time.

The creationist believes that all forms of life came into being by a creative act of the Creator-God in six days some six thousand years ago followed by a universal flood.

The two beliefs: (a) natural processes of evolution over many millions of years; and (b) supernatural creative processes in one week and a universal flood as recently as a few thousand years ago, are not compatible.

The evolutionist explanation is that most widely held in the west. A combination of that explanation with an intervention by God to set things off and guide in the process is the view most widely held in Christian circles. The creationist's view is widely held but still by a minority of those who call themselves Christian. The confusion caused by the different interpretations of the Bible is explained in Chapter 8.

The biblical creationist has two lines of defence: Negatively, the absence of contradictory evidence, and, positively, the Bible and confirmatory evidence.

The absence of contradictory evidence

Increasingly, since the publication of Charles Darwin's *Origin of Species* in 1859, the Theory of Evolution proposed by Darwin and expanded since, has been generally accepted as the explanation for the appearance of all forms of life—animal and vegetable.

The atheistic 'theory of evolution' presupposes a totally scientific environment in which 'evolution' is so self-evident that it requires no proof. The creationist is not limited to the scientific environment. The 'theory of evolution' is, therefore, open to the requirement of proof.

The theory of evolution rests, metaphorically speaking, on two legs . If these two legs can be proved or demonstrated to fulfil the requirements of scientific investigation, then the theory of evolution is an *explanatory one*. If the claims of these two legs cannot be substantiated, then the theory is *hypothetical* and is either accepted or rejected on grounds other than wholly scientific.

The following evidence of the unsustainability of the evolutionary theory uses the word in its *hypothetical* sense as understood by those working in the 'natural plus extra-natural' environment. It will make nonsense to those working exclusively in the 'natural' environment.

Leg 1   The evolution of self-reproducing cells

Part 1 of the first leg of the theory of evolution claims that, at some point in the distant past, the universe came into being in some more compact form that it is today, and that it has expanded and evolved into its present state. The events which have brought about the present situation of the galaxies and of any life-forms which exist on any of its celestial bodies, have occurred as a result of wholly natural forces. The existence of everything can be explained without reference to any supernatural force or intelligence.

Part 2 of the first leg of the evolutionary theory claims that, at some point many millions of years ago, in suitable conditions, some complex molecules evolved into living cells. This means that the living cells became able to reproduce themselves *and* to reproduce in themselves the reproducing mechanisms which gave rise to them.

Both creationists and evolutionists agree that the coming into being of the universe is beyond human verification. Neither the evolutionist's claim that the universe had a natural beginning, nor the creationist's claim that it was created by a supernatural power and intelligence, can be proved scientifically. There is no way of knowing what the situation was before the universe came into being, if, indeed there was a 'before' it existed.

Part 2 is different. The theory of evolution requires that complex molecules be transformed into living cells, that is, organisms which are able to reproduce themselves and the means of continuing that reproduction.

Experiments, such as those of S L Miller in 1953, have shown that under certain experimentally controlled conditions, using high energy radiations, a controlled mixture of methane, ammonia and hydrogen will transform into amino acids of which living cells are composed.

No one has yet been able to go further and either replicate or propose conditions which would produce living cells from inorganic compounds either in the laboratory or naturally. The current evolutionist's view is that the components and conditions for life existed on some celestial body from which that life found a suitable environment on earth.

Three quotations from scientific sources spell-out the nature of the problem:

"By the end of the nineteenth century, there was general agreement that life cannot arise from the non-living under conditions that now exist on our planet."
David Kirk *Biology Today* 1975

"The origin of the genetic code is the most baffling aspect of the problem of the origins of life, and a major conceptual or experimental breakthrough may be needed before we can make any substantial progress."
Leslie Orgel *Darwinism at the very beginning of life.*
New Scientist Vol 94 p.151

"There is one step that far outweighs the others in enormity: the step from macromolecules to cells. All other steps can be accounted for on theoretical grounds—if not correctly, at least elegantly. However, the macromolecule to cell transition is a jump of fantastic dimensions, which lies beyond the range of testable hypothesis."
Green and Goldberger *Molecular insights into the living process.*
(1967) pp 406-407

While the evolution from macromolecule to living cell has not been proved or demonstrated to be impossible, there appears to be no scientific evidence to date to prove or demonstrate in convincing terms that it is possible. No one has yet proposed conditions, on this planet or anywhere else in the universe, which, if they existed, would produce living cells from non-living molecules.

It is not the chemical components of living forms which set the problem. These have been identified. The problems lie in the very complex patterns in which those components are arranged and the conditions under which those arrangements can come about.

The idea of 'spontaneous generation', that is, the evolution of living cells from naturally occurring molecules, presupposes that everything in the universe is the result of interacting matter according to known natural laws. So far no one has yet been able to show how this was or could be achieved. It is clear now that if spontaneous generation is the explanation for the appearance of life, it must have happened elsewhere in the universe where the conditions were appropriate.

The spontaneous origin of life, as a leg on which stands the theory of evolution is, therefore, rejected on scientific grounds.

The leg does not exist.

Leg 2 The evolution of living cells from one state of complexity to another.

The second leg on which stands the 'theory of evolu-tion' relates to the proposed process of living organisms 'evolving' from one level of complexity to that of greater complexity. The theory proposes that all forms of life have evolved from simple to more complex forms by a process of many small stages over long periods of time.

For this theory to have scientific credibility, it must be possible to demonstrate that a living organism of one level of complexity can evolve into one of greater complexity. This process is widely ascribed to a combination of 'random mutation' and 'natural selection'.

According to this explanation, 'random mutation' produces life forms of greater complexity, and 'natural selection' determines which life-forms survive.

It is not difficult to accept that, given a range of life-forms, 'natural selection' will determine which survive. There are many examples of life-forms—animal and vegetation, of which a selection has continued to exist because of the ability of its members to survive the conditions of the environment. Darwin demonstrated this process relative to the finch species of birds. Moths have been subjected to a similar investigation. 'Natural selection' has been shown to apply.

The process of producing 'similar complexity' variations within cross-fertilizing species is well known and the *explanatory theory* for it is well established

The fundamental question, on the answer to which this second leg of the 'theory of evolution' depends, is this: Is it possible for one form of life to evolve into another more complex one?   If this is possible, the theory is supported by this leg.

If not, not!

Factors pointing to an evolution between species:

At this point it is worth summarizing the evidence for an evolution of life-forms from one level of complexity to a higher level. It is, in fact, necessary to understand this evidence in order to recognize that, presenting the evolutionist explanation is not simply an atheistic ploy to avoid the conclusions of science.

There are significant similarities not only between CF but also between NCF species.

(a) All forms of life are composed of the same chemical elements and there are many living cells which are common to many species of animal and plant life. For example, the composition of the genome of the ape is 98.5% the same as that of a human being

(b) There are many physical structures which are common to many species even though cross-fertilization between them is impossible. The similar type of hand/paw/claw which many tree-climbing animal species possess is an example of this. These similarities point to a possible causal link between them.

(c) There are many physical processes which are common across a variety of species. An example of this is the egg-laying and hatching reproductive process common to a number of animals and birds of different species from turtles to eagles. It would seem natural to suppose that there was some evolutionary link between them.

(d) All living forms require the same conditions for life such as the presence of oxygen, sun light, temperate temperatures and similar sources of nutrients to maintain life. The process of photosynthesis is common to many species.

(e) Similarities in fossil evidence suggest that some species are intermediate links between different species. This occurs when parts of the fossils of two different NCF species appear to be very similar. It is sometimes difficult to distinguish between the fossilized bones of similar cat-like animals.

(f) Some species have biological features which do not appear to contribute to the life of that life-form. These suggest that some organisms have evolved from previous life-forms in ways which make those features unnecessary and hence residual.

(g) At one time, similarities at different stages of the development of the foetus of an animal was considered to be evidence of the evolutionary path of that animal.

(h) Some characteristics of 'variations' between some CF species are similar to those of proposed products of evolution between NCF species.

Much research is being carried out to determine the paths by which these similarities in structures and functions may be linked. The results of this research is sufficient to convince many scientists that, in time, the whole story of the claimed evolution of species will be told in terms of totally natural causes. There is no need, therefore, to resort to some supernatural intervention to explain what is self-evident, even if not fully explained.

Factors which counter the theory of the evolution of species of animal and plant life:

These fall into two categories:

(a) General factors—those which are applicable to the whole range of life-forms, and

(b) 'Bridge' factors—those which relate to the 'bridges' or intermediate stages in the so-called evolution from one particular life-form to another.

General factors.
(1) The unchanging chromosome pairing

Chromosomes are complex molecules in the genes cells which determine the characteristics of the body carrying them. Normally, male and female chromosomes occur in matching pairs. At fertilization the genes cells in animals— male sperm and female egg, and at pollination in plants— pollen and stigma, the male chromosomes link with the matching female chromosomes and a new pairing takes place to form a new cell.

The pairing of chromosomes in the embryo stage of development remains unchanged throughout the life-time of the animal or plant. Passing on genes in this way is the natural process which produces the variations of the same species which exist today.

It is impossible, therefore, for any experience of an animal or plant to change the genes it passes on to the next generation. Science has failed to show how any natural activity or circumstance of an animal or plant can bring about 'mutations' in the fundamental biological structure.

2) Conditions for life

All animal and plant forms require suitable conditions for the maintenance of life. Air, sun light, heat and water are necessary for all forms of life. Some species of animal and plant life, however, require special conditions without which they cannot exist. Some depend on other forms of life for food. Such are predatory animals and insects, parasites and viruses which live on other life-forms,

In every case, if certain species developed, by whatever means, they would be eliminated if the appropriate sources of their nutrition were not available. This interdependence of life-forms—vegetation and animal, requires an order in their evolution and in that of their sources of nutrition.

(3) Minimum or irreducible complexity

There are in many forms of life, particularly in animal and bird life, mechanisms which work perfectly in their existing state but which would not work in less-than-perfect forms of the mechanism.

Such mechanisms are the human eye and heart, the wing of a bird and the defensive means of some insects and reptiles. There has been and there is today, considerable investigation into the mechanisms which maintain life, both internally in the body, and externally related to the conditions of living. Such scientific investigation includes possible evolutionary paths from one apparently irreducible complex biological mechanism to another of equal or greater complexity.

For instance, the mechanism by which the flow of blood is maintained throughout the body of a giraffe would not be necessary if, at an earlier stage of its evolution, its neck was much shorter. Clearly a biological change in the structure of the neck would have been necessary.

The human eye is possibly the most amazingly complex organ of the human body. No one has yet been able to construct a path by which simpler mechanisms could have existed which could 'evolve' into the human eye as it is now and still function effectively.

The 'bridge' which requires mutations to produce progressively complex irreducible mechanisms in evolving species between which there is no cross-fertilization is a big one indeed.

Science has not yet crossed this bridge.

(4) Instinct

There is a great deal of evidence for instinctive behaviour in many, if not all forms of animal life. Some of this behaviour is so essential that, without it, life would be impossible.

Many animals and birds breed in one part of the world, migrate elsewhere, often thousands of miles away, then return to the same location for breeding. Navigating very long distances is attributed to instinct. Bees and pigeons fly long distances for food and return unerringly to their starting point. Birds reduce the energy of movement by flying in formation at specific distances from each other to benefit from the leading bird's slip-stream. Every species of bird makes the same structure nest in similar situations. Turtles congregate to lay their eggs in sand with no known timing mechanism.

No one has yet worked out how 'evolving' species of animal and bird life could acquire ranges of abilities without which they could not survive.

(5) Mutation

A mutation is an alteration in the fundamental biological structure of a life-form. This is not to be confused with the variations produced by cross-fertilization, that is, the changes brought about in the genome by the pairing of chromosomes.

A mutation is occasional and cannot be predicted. The theory of evolution proposes that, although only occasional in terms of ordinary life-spans, millions of mutations have occurred over many millions, if not billions of years.

Experiments have been conducted to subject a small fruit fly—Drosophia melanogaster—to a variety of conditions—heat, X- and Gamma rays and other agents. Every mutation has produced distorted forms of the original fly. Not one mutation has proved to be advantageous in any way. Other experiments have produced similar results.

There is a great deal of research now into genetic engineering. 'Mutations' can be produced by the manipulation of cell structures. All these require the setting up by specialists of intervention procedures in appropriate conditions. No *natural* conditions have, as yet, been demonstrated to produce advantageous changes in the biological structure of any species of animal or plant.

The argument that what is not possible in the short historical period of human experience is possible in the millions of years of varied conditions on planet earth is one of belief rather than assured scientific knowledge.

(6) Intelligent design

A major objection to the theory of evolution between non-cross fertilizing species lies in the arrangement of the components of the genome of animals and plants.

Two factors are involved: the physical components of the genome and the arrangement of those components.

As has already been pointed out, the basic chemical constituents of the biological cells of all living organisms are the same. The obvious evidence for this lies in the very similar residue which results from the decomposition of all dead life-forms. It is supported by the chemical analysis of all animal and plant life. There is convincing biological evidence that the chief differences between species is not in the composition of their genomes, but in their design.

To illustrate this, compare the front page of any two daily newspapers. The composition, in terms of the paper and ink used, will be almost identical. The major difference between the two papers will be the nature of the news and the words reporting it. The fundamental difference is one of design, not of composition .

The vast amount of research into the biological structure of living organisms reveals the great complexity of their genomes.   Science has so far failed to demonstrate how the design of the components of the genome of one species can change in design into that of another non-cross fertilizing species by a process of 'random mutations'.

(7) The age of the earth.

A clear difference in the claims of the evolutionist and the creationist is centred on the time factor. The creationist claims that creation took place in six days. The evolutionist claims that the evolutionary process and the laying down of geological strata took millions of years. This 'old earth' claim is, in fact, an integral part of the evolutionary theory.

The proof of a 'young earth' would demolish the theory of evolution. The question is, therefore. what is the evidence that the universe, including planet earth is millions, if not billions, of years old?

There are two categories of evidence:

(a) *Fossils in sedimentary and rock strata.*

This method of linking dating of geological periods with the fossil remains has been largely discounted as it is based on circular reasoning. The age of strata is determined by the age of the fossils found in them, and the age of fossils is determined from the age of the strata in which they are found. The only thing of which one can be sure, is that the fossils are of the same age as the strata in which they are found.

It is further assumed that sedimentary strata have required millions of years to assume their present form. This has been challenged by the recent experience of sedimentary layers with similar features being formed by rivers caused by recent volcanic action. Also, rocks showing a very old radio-metrically calculated age, have been found with fossils embedded in them of a much more recent age.

(b) *Radio-metric dating*

This is based on the fact that when certain radio-active compounds are embedded in bones of dead animals, rocks or plants, their radio-activity decays into a 'daughter' compound. By comparing the radio-activity of the free compounds with those of the so-called 'daughter' compound, it is possible to work out the time lapse between the original and 'daughter' compounds. This calculation is based on the fact that, given the same conditions over the whole period of time, the 'half-life' of a radio-active compound is known.

The radio-active compounds most frequently used are derivatives of Uranium, Thorium and Potassium.

For a radio-metric measurement to be reliable, it must be possible to be sure which is being measured— the 'original' or the 'daughter' element. It is fundamental to ensure that the rocks or fossils in question have not been subject to any major upheavals, such as volcanic action, and that the conditions of the earth's magnetic force, force of gravity, and time, have remained constant throughout the period in question. Given these certainties, it is assumed that the rate of decay of radio-active elements is constant and has been so for millions of years.

The problem is put into perspective by an illustration. To extrapolate the experimental findings over a few thousand years of time to millions of years is like tracing the trajectory of a bullet fired from a gun. To claim that a bullet, which hits a target at 100 metres, would hit a similar target millions of kilometres away would only be credible if the conditions were the same throughout the trajectory.

Further doubt is raised by the often greatly different radio-metric datings obtained when using different radio-active elements. Great differences have also been recorded for the age of similar rocks found in different parts of the world using the same radio-metric measuring means.

The unreliability of radio-metric measurements is made worse by the fact that some fossil remains of animal or plant life, claimed to have evolved at a late date in their evolutionary path, are found in strata which radio-metric measurements claim were laid down millions of years before. The variations in measurement amount to millions of years.

Radio-metric dating has proved to be a very useful tool in measurements of age within recorded history, but very unreliable in determining the age of fossils, rocks and sedimentary strata of a seemingly much greater age.

'Bridge' factors

To illustrate the evolutionary claim, imagine that to evolve from one species into another to be like crossing a bridge across a river.

The 'bridge' between species which are capable of cross-fertilization, that is CF species, is well established. This 'bridge' is regularly crossed by dog, cat and horse breeders and by horticulturists producing variations of flowers, fruit trees and vegetables.

The 'bridge' between species of animal or plant-life between which there is no cross-fertilization or cross-pollination, that is NCF species, is different.

To continue the 'bridge' metaphor, there are probably several thousand rivers in the world. If I were to claim that there are no bridges across any of those rivers, you would, rightly, think me mad, blind or, at best, ill-informed. If someone were to challenge that claim, they could easily show it to be false by taking me to a nearby bridge. The existence of one bridge would shatter my claim.

It is estimated that there are more than 10 million non-cross-fertilizing species. So far, no one has yet demonstrated, either in replicable practice or theoretically, that an evolution has taken place or can take place between any two of them. A scientifically provable evolutionary 'bridge' across any two of the millions of NCF species would shatter any claim that evolution is impossible.

The general factors which point to the unsustainability of the theory of evolution are supported by other evidence. In the chain from simple cells to the most complex—from amoeba to human beings, for instance, there are a number of 'bridges' which present particular problems. These relate to the biological structural changes required in the evolution of one category of animal or plant life to another. These 'bridges' appear to be uncrossable.

(1) Macromolecule to the simplest cells

The bridge from inorganic complex molecule to the simplest living cells presents a particular problem which has already been discussed. The simplest living cells: *amoeba, paramecium* and *euglena*, are very complex and very different from each other. It has, so far, been impossible to propose an evolutionary path from complex molecule to any one of these simple cells. Nor has it been possible to suggest one or more simpler forms of any of them from which all three could have evolved separately. There appears to be nothing simpler than the known simplest, nor an evolutionary path between the simplest cells.

This 'bridge' has not yet been crossed

(2) Invertebrates to vertebrates

95% of all animals are invertebrates, that is, they have no backbone. There are 47,000 species of vertebrates—with backbone.

The distinguishing feature of vertebrate species is that they possess segmented back-bones. Movement is achieved by each segment of the backbone being so shaped and connected to the next that it moves smoothly one against the other. The invertebrate species nearest to vertebrates have a continuous spinal column.

The 'bridge' from invertebrate to vertebrate is a massive one. There are some species of sea-going life which do not have a back-bone which are similar to sea-going life with a back-bone. The nature and the structure of the back-bones and spinal columns of these life-forms may appear to behave in similar ways, but their differences defy a scientific explanation in terms of an evolution from one to the other. Both the spinal columns of invertebrates and the back-bones of vertebrates appear to be so efficient that to evolve into another form appears very unnecessary.

The similarities between these species are remarkable, but no one has found living forms or fossils from which it has been possible to work out how the more complex segmented back-bone could have evolved from the less complex continuous sinuous form. Here again, the difference between the two is that of design. The invertebrates to vertebrates 'bridge' has not yet been crossed.

(3) Sexual dimorphism

In the move upwards from the complex to the more complex, there is gap between self-reproducing life-forms and those which require two different forms—male and female to complete the reproductive process. The species on one side of this 'bridge' are referred to as 'single sex' and, on the other, 'bisexual'.

No one has yet demonstrated how one form, with all its reproductive organs in itself, became two forms—male and female, with their reproductive organs divided between them. The evolutionary process requires the separation of the physical organs of reproduction, the acquisition of the physical means of the one fertilizing the other, and the maintenance of life while the male and female are in the process of evolving.

In animal life-forms, there are many different mechanisms of fertilization, processes of pregnancy, incubation of eggs and larvae in the great variety of bisexual life-forms, from the egg-laying bird to the metamorphosis of the butterfly.

The sexual reproductive process in animal life-forms, is dependent on the proximity of the male and female sexual organs and does not usually depend on a third party. In plant reproduction, the fertilization process often requires a third party—bees, birds or other insects, to transfer the male pollen to the female organ.

It has been impossible even to hypothesize intermediate stages between 'single-sex' organisms and 'bisexual forms. No one has yet demonstrated how the development from 'single sex' life-forms to bisexual life-forms evolved or could have evolved.

This bridge has not yet been crossed.

(4) From fish to amphibian

In the science explanation of evolution, land-forms of life evolved from sea-living life. An intermediate form is the amphibian. There are species which, as the name suggests, have the ability to move both in water and on land. However, the structure of the leg of, say a newt, an amphibian, is so different from the fin of, say a dolphin, a sea-going fish, that it has proved impossible even to propose a path of evolution from one to the other.

This is an example of the claimed ability of species of animal life to acquire fundamental changes to their biological structures by a change of environment or by a different use of limbs, fins or other parts of the body.

The similarity between some fins of fish and some legs of amphibians, suggests that there might be an evolutionary link between them, but science has not yet demonstrated how this could have been achieved.

That 'bridge' has not yet been crossed.

(5) From amphibian to reptile.

The similarities between some amphibians and some reptiles are obvious and possible paths of evolution from one to the other are not beyond the imagination. However, there are very significant differences and it is these which appear to make a 'bridge' across them impossible.

Amphibians, such as frogs, lay their eggs in water and the path to maturity requires passing through the stage of tadpole. Reptiles, such as lizards, lay hard-shelled eggs from which, after incubation, young reptiles emerge immediately replicas of the adults.

There may be a similarity between frogs and lizards, but the development of their organs and processes of reproduction have so far defied a proposed evolutionary path.

This bridge has not yet been crossed.

(6) Reptiles to mammals.

The 'bridge' from reptile to mammal would appear to be the shortest and most easily crossable as there are some reptiles which are not immediately distinguishable from mammals. For instance, both have similar jaws.

The wide variety of reptiles: alligators, crocodiles, lizards, snakes and turtles provide problems to form evolutionary paths between themselves. Equally, mammals appear in very diverse forms: whales, seals and porpoises are sea-going examples; bats move in the air, and polar bears, monkeys, pigs, cats and opossums live on land.

No one has yet proposed a generally recognized evolutionary path for either all the reptiles or all the mammals. Even further from current theory is the transition from reptile to mammal.

This 'bridge' has not yet been crossed.

(7) Animals to birds

Some fish and animals have wing-like structures which enable them to glide from wave to wave or from branch to branch of trees. There are some birds, such as the ostrich and the penguin. which have wings but which cannot fly.

The wing of a bird is a remarkably complex structure yet there are many different variations in the great variety of birds which exist in the world, all of which appear to achieve their function of flying with maximum efficiency.

The structure of the wing of a bird is so perfectly adapted to flight that anything less would result in either a failure to fly or elimination by 'natural selection'.

The ostrich and the penguin suggest that they could be part of an evolutionary process in which the wings have not developed sufficiently to fly, nor so inadequately as to warrant elimination by 'natural selection'.

Those fish or animals which have wing-like structures which allow them to glide from wave to wave or from tree to tree, are clearly either fish or animals. They have not yet been fitted into the intermediate stages of evolution from one to the other.

The 'bridge' from animals to birds has so far proved to be uncrossable.

(8) The bi-valve to the avian lung.

A particular feature of birds provides special problems. Animals have a lung in which air is breathed in and out by the same air passages: it is *bi-directional.* In birds, air is breathed in at one end of the lung and expelled from the other: it is *uni-directional.* It would be very inefficient for birds to breathe out against their direction of flight.

The difference in the biological structure of the unidirectional breathing mechanism of a bird from that of a bi-directional breathing mechanism of an animal is great. It is difficult to imagine what path the evolution from animal-to bird-lung could take. The only possibility could lie if a mutation produced a small aperture at the rear end of the animal-lung which progressively evolved into a larger aperture culminating in the unidirectional avian lung. This also supposes that intermediate forms would be sufficiently efficient to avoid 'natural elimination'.

The 'bridge' from *bi-directional* to *avian* lung has not yet been crossed.

(9) Ape to human

The biggest 'bridge' which no one has yet been able to cross, in scientific terms, is that between the ape and human beings. The human brain is much bigger than that of any ape. The bone structure of the human female is very much bigger than that of a female ape which makes possible the passing at birth of a bigger head. A person is able to walk upright in a way that no ape can. The functioning of the reproductive organs of apes and humans is similar but there are striking differences. Not only is the brain bigger in humans than in apes, but it is capable of vastly greater activities—thinking, manual dexterity, consciousness of themselves and a moral conscience.

There have been many claims to have discovered 'missing links' in the evolutionary path from ape to 'man'. To date, there is no fossil record nor a replicable process nor a theoretical scientific path by which a human being could evolve from an ape.

Recent research into the structure and functioning of the human and ape genomes reveals great differences, not in the composition of their components, but in their biological design. No means has been suggested by which this design could be altered by natural processes unless the 'natural selection' of millions of 'random mutations' over millions of years can be referred to as a natural process. Scientific literature on this evolutionary step assumes that it took place.

The 'bridge' between ape and human being is the biggest of all the 'bridges' because the human being has features which occur nowhere else in the natural world—consciousness, ability to think, verbal communication, moral awareness. No bridge between ape and human being has yet been found nor has one been proposed within the limits of the 'natural' environment.

Conclusions:

The two legs on which the 'theory of evolution' stands are unsustainable. That 'life' could have evolved from 'non-life' is still a scientific mystery for which there is no credible evidence. The 'evolution' from one of the many millions of species to another between which there is no cross-fertilization defies all scientific explanation. These 'bridges' have proved to be uncrossable.

There is only one environment in which it is possible to claim with scientific assurance that the 'theory of evolution' is a valid explanation for the appearance of all life-forms, and that is the 'natural' environment. To those thinking and working exclusively in this environment, the, to them, self-evident fact of the absence of any other possible explanation, makes the 'theory of evolution' an *explanatory* one and hence closed to any investigation which might challenge its *explanatory* claim, and suggest that it might be considered as a *hypothetical* one.

An important conclusion from this reasoning on the part of evolutionists, is that, if the evolutionary theory is *not* true, then their atheist position is untenable. There must be some other explanation requiring some intervention outside the 'natural' environment. Looked at in this way, the unsubstantiated claim of the atheistic evolutionist, is a very powerful argument for some supernatural intervention.

Far from closing the door to an investigation of a true explanation of the appearance of the universe and of all life-forms, it opens the door to another possibility, that of a powerful, intelligent, supernatural being who created people and revealed to them *how*, *when* and, above all, *why* He acted as He did.

Chapter 7

The creationist's case
The Bible and confirming evidence

The negative defence of the creationist rests on the inability of secular humanist atheists to substantiate in scientific terms the claims of the evolutionary explanation of the origins of the universe and the life-forms in it.

The positive case for the creation origin of the universe and all life-forms in it rests squarely on the Christian's faith in the truth of the Bible account. The defence lies in two stages:

The first line of defence is by the creationist in the face of the claims of the evolutionist, whether atheist or Christian. The second lies in the defence of the creationist in the face of the claims of the Christian evolutionist. This latter defence will be presented in the next chapter.

The assured findings of science which corroborate the biblical record.

There is no scientifically verifiable evidence which proves that the universe and the life-forms in it were the creation of a supernatural 'God'. However, there is evidence that the details and order in which creation and the early history of the world is recorded in the Bible is corroborated by science. Equally, there is no scientific evidence which confirms that a universal flood took place within recorded history, but there is demonstrable evidence that it happened.

(a) A single beginning.

It is one of the achievements of recent scientific investigation to conclude that the universe had a beginning. Before that, it was considered that the universe was infinite—it has always been there. Later a theory was developed which proposed that, as the celestial galaxies moved apart so new galaxies were continually forming, thus ensuring a 'steady state'.

There is no universal agreement among scientists as to the nature of the beginning of the universe but they are in no doubt that it happened. In layman's language it is the 'Big Bang'. The movements of galaxies of stars leaves no doubt that the universe is expanding, hence, it is argued, there must have been a point when the expansion began. However, the only sure deduction from the evidence is that the universe has not always been as it is now.

While science confirms that there was a 'beginning', and there are hypothetical theories of its progress to its present state, science has no explanation as to how it came about. Science only confirms the first three words of the event recorded in the first sentence of the Bible: *"In the beginning, God created the heavens and the earth."*

(b) The 'kinds' or species of life-forms

The Genesis record is quite specific: God created all life-forms 'after their kinds'. This implies that life-forms did not appear by an evolutionary process, and that all development of species is within their 'kinds'. 'Kinds' being species within which there is cross-fertilization.

Scientific evidence confirms the precise nature of the expression 'after their kinds'. The processes by which animal and plant life reproduce themselves within their 'kinds' are assured findings of science. Scientific evidence also confirms that there is no reproduction of life-forms outside their 'kind'.

Furthermore, the order in which the different 'kinds' were created demonstrates an order which is supported by scientific evidence—vegetation before animal and bird life.

(c) Human beings traced to one source

Recent research into the development of the genome of human beings shows that there was, at some point in the past, a common origin, an original male and female pair. This finding provides no evidence of how the original male and female came into existence, but it confirms the biblical record that 'God created man—male and female' and that, after the universal flood, the world was populated by the descendants of Noah and his wife. Given that fact, Noah's wife must be, after Eve, the most significant woman of antiquity, both historically and scientifically.

As all human beings can be traced to one ancestor, this confirms the biblical record that God created the first man and woman as fully matured adults. Evolution would have produced many intermediate stages between apes and human beings, the fossils of which would have been discoverable. There is no contradiction here between science and the Bible.

(d) The appearance of civilizations within recent history.

Scientists are not agreed as to when the claimed evolution of human beings occurred but the proposed dates are millions of years ago. During the intervening years there would have been many intermediate stages slowly producing increasing levels of the kind of awareness and mental abilities which are features of people now.

It is surprising, therefore, that, less than 10,000 years ago, there appeared on the earth several civilizations of people each with their own language, many with their own systems of writing. Such were the Hittites, the Babylonians, the Egyptians, the Assyrians, the Mayans, and the Chinese. Some possessed intellectual abilities which enabled them to 'read the stars', form their own calendars and build large and complex buildings such as the Babylonian Ziggurats, the Egyptian pyramids, Stone Henge and a host of other constructions.

All this is evidence of a relatively sudden appearance of people on the earth, with highly developed mental abilities and skills. This does not prove the biblical record, but it is strong evidence that that record is more reliable than the evolutionary hypothesis. History confirms that human beings were not originally primitive ape-like hominids which gradually developed into the intelligent people they are today. Rather, this evidence confirms that people have only inhabited this earth for several thousand years and that they were originally, as intelligent as they are today. No one has yet been able to work out exactly on what mathematical bases the Egyptian pyramids were built nor how the massive blocks of stone were raised to form Stone Henge.

The evidence of archeology points to the appearance of human beings on the earth as being not earlier than 10,000 years ago. That supports the biblical record.

(e) Geological strata demonstrated to have taken place in a very short space of time.

The recorded effects of floods within living memory demonstrate that canyons, such as the Grand Canyon in the USA, could have been produced in a very short space of time. The claimed erosion causing canyons and the laying down of sedimentary strata over millions of years could have been produced within a few weeks by the great forces released by the vast volumes of water that covered the earth in the biblical flood.

It was claimed that the reduction of forests to coal, found in distinct layers, required millions of years. It has been shown that wood, when subject to intense heat and vibration, as in volcanoes and earthquakes, can be converted into carbon in minutes.

None of this evidence proves that the earth is 'young' but there is growing scientific evidence which demonstrates that it is not necessarily 'old'.

Conclusions

(a) The scientific evidence for the 'Big Bang' as an initial event in the history of the universe confirms the biblical timing of creation: *'In the beginning, God created the heavens and the earth.'*

Science provides no clear evidence of how the 'Big Bang' took place. Theoretically reversing the evident expansion of the universe leads to the conclusion that everything there is now was once compressed into zero size and was infinitely hot—concepts which defy the imagination of most people, even scientists. This points to the creationist's understanding of the biblical record that, as the first 'man' was created in an adult form with a built-in appearance of history, so the universe was created with a built-in appearance of expansion from a 'Big Bang'.

(b) Science confirms that all forms of life appear in some 'kinds' or grouping, each distinct from all others. The evolution of one species into another by any means other than by cross-fertilization between species has not yet been proved possible. The claim that 'the evolution of species' is self-evident and only needs further research to explain the process, is only sustainable in an environment in which there is no activity which is not attributable to wholly natural causes.

(c) The scientific research into the human DNA demonstrates that all human beings can be traced to one original pair. This confirms the biblical statement that God *'made from one blood all nations of men to settle on the face of the earth.'* [1] This runs counter to the evolutionary model of many intermediate stages with many sub-humans whose survival was determined by 'natural selection'.

(d) Science has shown that if the surface of the earth were level, there is sufficient water to cover its surface to a depth of several hundred metres. The separation of the continents and the raising of mountain ranges could have been produced by a combination of great volcanic earth upheavals and the fall of rain from a melting ice canopy to produce the results which science claims took millions of years.

Although 'creation' and a universal flood cannot be proved scientifically to have happened, it is, nevertheless, not demonstrably contradicted by scientific evidence.

The creationist's negative defence lies in the absence of assured findings of science which make impossible the plain simple interpretation of biblical statements:

(i) God created the universe, people and all forms of life according to their 'kinds' in six days;

(ii) God brought about a great flood over the earth which left the rock formations and sedimentary strata very much as they are today.

[1] Acts 17:26

Chapter 8

The creationist's case
The Bible & the unrecognized confusion

The case for the creationist's understanding of the origins of the universe and of all life-forms in it rests foundationally on the Genesis record in the Bible. This the secular humanist atheist evolutionist cannot accept. It follows that he or she cannot understand the Christian's faith in the biblical record. The presuppositions in the minds of those who think exclusively in the 'natural' environment preclude an understanding of anything which, for them, is not in the 'real' world.

Similarly, the creationist, who thinks exclusively in the 'extra-natural' environment cannot understand the confidence that evolutionists have in their claims. It is necessary to understand the boundaries of the 'natural world' as defined by the atheist, in order to understand his convictions.

For the reasons given in the forgoing chapters, the creationist's and evolutionist's attempts to understand each other's positions are fraught with the consequence of undefined words and misunderstood environments. This inevitably leads to confusion.

However, the confusion does not end there. There is further confusion among Christians in their understanding of the biblical record of creation and the great flood..

There are, broadly speaking, four groupings of Christians in their interpretation of the biblical records:

(a) The unthinking:

Most Christians appear to accept the Genesis record of creation and the great flood without giving any thought to whether those events were historical or ideas in a parable, allegory or myth. There appears to be little realization of the extent to which the major biblical truths concerning Jesus Christ, the salvation offered to men and women and the principles of behaviour of Christians in society, are founded in the events recorded in Genesis. Or, if they understand the source of these truths, they are prepared to accept them without questioning the nature of their source and, hence, their authority.

(b) Those who think in 'separate compartments' of the mind.

There are Christians who consider that science and religion are totally separate spheres of reality which, metaphorically, occupy separate compartments of the mind. Science is related to the 'natural' world of physical objects and forces; religion is related to ideas. It is, therefore, quite wrong to mix the two. The reasoning required for 'evolution', a physical process, and that for 'creation', a religious idea, cannot be entertained in the mind at the same time and can, therefore, never come into conflict.

[1] 1 Peter 3:15

(c) Christian evolutionists:

The wide acceptance of the 'theory of evolution', and hence, of an 'old earth', in the secular world leads Christian evolutionists to interpret the biblical record so that it does not appear to contradict the claimed findings of science. Scientific evidence is sufficiently strong for them to replace the plain meaning of the Bible record with their alternative meanings. Science overrides or modifies the God-given revelation to conform to generally accepted scientific ideas.

(d) Creationists:

Creationists accept the Genesis record as being literally true in the sense that the words used have the plain simple meanings as would be understood by a contemporary Hebrew reader or a reader of the time when Jesus and the Apostles quoted from it. Some words have an historical meaning, e.g. 'day', or a symbolic meaning, e.g. 'one flesh'. The simple meaning of words is defined by the context.

In order to maintain the authority of the Bible, many Christians modify their understanding of the biblical record to make it compatible with science. The result is the opposite to that desired. The credibility of the Bible is diminished and its message clouded by confusion.

The well-known Professor Richard Dawkins has made an interesting contribution to this situation by suggesting that those who combine the theory of evolution with that of biblical creation are really dishonest.

According to him, anyone who recognizes the validity of the evolution explanation of the origin of life-forms must reject any other. They are, therefore, atheists, even if they do not admit the fact. Those who claim to be Christians and accept the theory of evolution as God initiated and God guided, are really creationists whose God is not big enough to do what He claims to have done.

We are inclined to agree with Professor Dawkins but for different motives. Nor do we go as far as he does in suggesting dishonesty in the reasoning.

The fact is, however, that the secular, humanist atheist evolutionist has a much more coherent defence than that presented by most Christians. The reason for this is simply that most Christians do not have a reasoned argument to present. They are confused or divided among themselves as to what they believe.

The sad effect of this confusion among Christians is that there is no unified Christian defence against the atheist's position. It is not surprising, therefore, that many atheists regard Christians as either blind, unthinking and unreasoning believers in religious fairy stories or misguided followers of superstitious ideas. While the Christian's defence of his or her faith is largely *experiential*, it offers little defence to those whose faith is largely *intellectual*.

Revelation and reason

The Bible is God's *revelation* of His mind, actions and purposes which would otherwise be unknown. Reason is the mental process we apply to the way we receive that revelation.

The issue is an important one: Does the Christian believe by using *reason informed by revelation*, or *revelation informed by reason*?

Which is the final authority: *revelation* or *reason*?

Here lies the basic difference between the Christian evolutionist and the creationist. The priority of the source of authority affects the interpretation of every biblical record of events, including creation.

Biblical illustrations:

(A) The most important truths of the Bible are stated in simple words whose meaning is clear:

The birth of Jesus: *"The virgin will be with child"*, [1]

Salvation: *"Christ died for our sins"* [2]

The resurrection of Jesus: *"He was raised on the third day."* [3]

All these facts are believed by Christians to be historically true because they are there in the Bible. None of them is scientifically verifiable in the sense that no one is alive today who witnessed the events which are the grounds for that faith. The Christian faith is founded on these historical facts as recorded in the Bible.

Also there in the Bible:

Creation: *"For in six days the LORD made the heavens and the earth, the sea, and all that is in them."* [4]

This is not accepted as being historically true by many Christians.

Why?

Reason dictates otherwise!

(B) The Apostle Paul wrote:

As in Adam all die, so in Christ all are made alive.[5]

This can be interpreted in three different ways which represent the views of the three categories of people:

The atheist:

*As in (**mythical**) Adam all die, so in (**mythical**) Christ all are made (**mythically**) alive.*

The Christian evolutionist:

*As in (**mythical**) Adam all die, so in (**historical**) Christ all are made (**historically**) alive.*

The Christian creationist:

*As in (**historical**) Adam all die, so in (**historical**) Christ all are made (**historically**) alive.*

[1] Isaiah 7:14   [2] 1 Corinthians 15:3   [3] 1 Corinthians 15:3   [4] Exodus 20:11   [5] 1 Corinthians 15:22

For the atheist, the stories of creation and the flood are fairy stories and their consequences mere superstition. Referring to them as 'myth' does little to raise them above the level of fantasy.

For the Christian, the Bible makes it clear that God's objective is that all should be made *historically* spiritually alive in Jesus Christ. The plain reading of the Genesis record is that Adam was an historical man and that his act of disobedience led to all his and Eve's descendants being born 'dead in sin' from that time to the present day. If the story of the fall of Adam and Eve is a myth, where does that place the biblical truth of the inherent, humanly communicated 'sinfulness' of every man and woman?

The priority of clarity

The biggest contributors to confusion are those who mix what they understand to be biblical teaching with what they understand to be the findings of science without checking the true meaning of biblical statements, nor the true state of scientific theories. The consequence of this is that many Christians who espouse evolution or subscribe to the 'old age' of the earth, do not present a recognized body of truth. They 'pick and choose' and modify the biblical record to make their Gospel acceptable to what they believe to be scientific thinking. In so doing, they diminish the authority of the book on which they base their faith.

The most frequent replies made to the author to questions relating to the biblical records of creation and the great flood have been along the lines:

"I am quite happy with treating the first eleven chapters of Genesis as a God-given myth; it does not affect my preaching the Gospel."

"I do not find it necessary to fight the scientific claim that this is an 'old earth'."

"I do not think that it makes any difference if Adam was an historical person or a character in a God-given myth."

"There are enough words in Genesis which are sufficiently vague in their meaning to allow both the creation and the evolution explanations."

"I think there are more important things in the Bible to argue over."

A serious ground of confusion lies in the positioning of the exact place in the biblical record where the myth becomes history. The most common position places the call of Abraham—Genesis 12:1 as the first historical event. All before that is mythical—a parable to illustrate truth.

The result in people's thinking is either to avoid facing facts, to leave the issues to the experts or ... *confusion.*

Such an approach to the biblical record supports the claim of many secular humanists that Christians are simply Bible-thumping promoters of fables and superstition.

The fairy story of Goldilocks and the three bears figures in the defence of evolutionists. It illustrates an important principle, that of 'natural selection'. However, it would be a foolish evolutionist who would go further and insist that, as Goldilocks was a little girl, all little girls should taste their porridge before eating it!

In a similar way, if the creation and great flood records are treated as Goldilocks-like stories—fables with a meaning, then their authority lies in the human interpreter rather than in God, their source. There are many human interpreters. It is no surprise that there are many interpretations of the biblical record. Stupid as it may sound, that is exactly how secular atheists interpret the defence of many Christians. They claim that all men and women are sinners by quoting what to them is a fairy story about a naked Adam and Eve and a fruit tree in an idyllic garden.

What is the difference between a fairy story and a myth?

The crucial factor

If you were to ask most Christians in the UK today:

"Why do you believe that 'God created the heavens and the earth?" the answer would probably be:

"Because I believe what the Bible says!"

Good! If you were to go a step further and ask:

"Why do you believe what the Bible says?" the answers would probably point to the place of the Bible in their lives, their very real relationship to the God of the Bible and the value of its moral principles for them and for society. Their belief in the biblical record stems from their experience of the life the Bible teaches.

The reasons are *experiential.*

Such reasons are good but insufficient. They are not strong enough to defend attacks on faith when experience is questioned. To return to the question above:

"Why do you believe what the Bible says?

Mature Christians would answer:

"Because it is God's word."

Good! But what does that mean? It is with the different meanings of that reply that confusion begins to appear.

"What is 'God's word'?

There are two answers which appear similar but are very different. Within these differences lie the source of great confusion in many people's minds.

(a) The Bible is God's word because it *contains* what God wants people to know. Every person is to read the Bible and interpret it in the light of their own experience and of other knowledge available to them—science and secular history. Biblical truth lies in the principles illustrated in the Bible and not in the actual words used. The original meanings of words are subject to modification in the light of later events and modern thinking.

That is the position of the *Christian evolutionist.*

(b) The Bible is God's word because it *is* what God wants people to know. That means that every word recorded there means what it meant in the language in which it was originally written at the time it was written or quoted elsewhere, irrespective of one's experience or of other available knowledge. It is God-breathed in that the words which convey the sense are as God 'breathed' them into the writers.

That is the position of the *creationist*.

The creationist's defence:

The defence of the Christian against all attacks from whatever quarter is dependent on his or her relationship to the Bible, and that, in turn depends on his or her relationship to the God of the Bible.

While the relationship of the creationist to the secular atheist evolutionist is of importance in defending the biblical truth of creation, the relationship of the creationist to the Christian evolutionist is of equal importance because therein lies the challenge to personal integrity, ability to face evolutionary challenges and effectiveness in proclaiming the Christian gospel and avoiding confusion.

Jesus stated His relationship to the Old Testament scriptures in no uncertain terms:

" *For verily I say unto you, till heaven and earth pass, one jot or one tittle shall in no wise pass from the law, till all be fulfilled.'* " [1]

A later version (ASV) brings the terms *'one jot or one tittle'* up to date: *"not the smallest letter or part of a letter"*

Nothing could be clearer. For Jesus, not one word, not even one letter of the 'Law of Moses' will ever be changed, modified, or given a different meaning from that originally intended. Genesis is the first book of the 'Law of Moses'. The strength of Jesus' statement suggests that He foresaw what some people would try to do to God's word,

[1] Matthew 5:18 (KJV)

The 'infallibility' and 'inerrancy' of the Bible

"All Scripture is God-breathed" [1] the Bible claims for itself, that is, while human hands wrote the words of the Bible, the source of those words is God. The writers of the over 40 sections of the Bible over a period of over 1500 years, may have written other documents, letters or poetry, but only those which form the Bible are the God-given expression of His revealed thinking and communication to the people He created. Every word of the Bible is there because God put it there and it means what God means it to mean.

It is to this claim for the Bible that the words 'infallibility' and 'inerrancy' refer. These are theological terms which usually only occur in theological colleges but understanding them is important and a simple understanding of them is possible.

"Infallible' means that the Bible communicates truthfully all that God wants people to know. Its meaning is always correct and without mistake.

"Inerrant' means that every word of the Bible is there as God wants it to be. Words can be used in historical records, allegorical, symbolical writings and in parables, but, in their context, the meanings of the words never err. They are inerrant.

Support for the verbal inspiration of the Bible and the Genesis record in particular.

The accusation is frequently made that the Christian who believes in the 'infallibility' and 'inerrancy' of the Bible is flying in the face of modern scholarship, secular historical evidence and the findings of modern science. They are accused of believing the unbelievable, of by-passing reason, and of living in their make-believe world in order to satisfy their narrow-minded, bigoted ideas.

[1] 2 Timothy 3:16

It is true that among the many millions of people who call themselves Christian in the world today, there are many strange ideas proposed which are claimed to originate in the Bible. It is the more important, therefore, that Christians be aware of the grounds for the sure faith that they place in the God-given Bible.

(1) Historical and scientific accuracy.

The Bible is not primarily a record of historical events. There are many important world events which are not mentioned in it. However, where there is a mention of an historical event or of a geographical location, there has been either evidence to support its accuracy or no evidence to deny the stated facts.

The Bible is not primarily a scientific treatise, but there is no statement there which the assured findings of science have demonstrated to be incorrect. The reverse is true. The prophet Isaiah wrote of 'the circle of the earth' many centuries before science proved that the earth was not a flat surface as many believed it to be. This claim for the accuracy of historical and scientific evidence cannot be made for any other ancient religious writing.

(2) The spiritual, moral and ethical basis of society

All the foundations of the spiritual, moral and ethical bases of Christian society depend on the authority of the Bible in its infallible and inerrant expression of God's mind. The roots of all these are to be found in Genesis. Jesus confirmed this by quoting from them. To deny the authenticity of the Genesis record is to reject the authority of God and to diminish the credibility of Jesus.

Human responsibility: God created man—male and female in His own image, man is responsible to Him above any human institution. Cain *is* his brother's keeper.

Abortion, capital punishment—God made 'man' in His image. To kill, that is, murder a 'man' is to destroy a person who is in 'God's image'.

divorce, homosexuality—God ordained the marriage of one man to one woman and hence sexual union between them, to be unique and exclude all other.

ecology—God gave to 'man' the responsibility for managing the earth's resources to the benefit of that and future generations.

dress—God made clothes so that the people He had created would not be naked. Dress was not simply to cover a naked person but to ensure the discipline of sexual behaviour: intimacy within and exclusion outside marriage.

evil—sin entered God's perfect world by one man therefore, all men are sinners. This is not a genetically inherited trait nor a philosophical idea but a spiritual state following an historical event. This forms a foundation truth of God's plan of salvation. To deny it is to deny the Gospel.

ancestors of Jesus—the first 23 ancestors of Jesus are recorded in Genesis. Their names figure again in the Gospel of Luke. To relegate these to mythology is to deny the genealogy of Jesus.

Satan: a created spirit-being, not a philosophical concept. An adversary of God, a 'liar from the beginning'

God's covenant with Noah—never to destroy the earth again by a flood.

Babel: the reason and purpose for the many languages of nations in the world.

Distribution of nations: The geographical distribution of the sons of Noah and the creation of the major population areas of the world.

Jesus coming again 'as in the days of' Noah and Lot— If the events of those days are mythical, then the coming again of Jesus is metaphorical!

To relegate the early chapters of Genesis to myth while retaining the rest as history is to deny the 'God-breathed' nature of the Bible and to reject God's final authority in issues of personal, social and moral conduct and to undermine His warnings of final judgement. God's 'good news' to the world is firmly grounded in the authenticity of the historical events recorded in Genesis.

(3) Biblical prophecy

The prophetic writings of the Bible have no parallel in any other writings in the world. No so-called 'god' of any other religion has foretold history before it happened. Many events, prophesied hundreds of years previously, have happened as predicted.

Here are some examples:

The Genesis record predicts that 'man' would be dominated by Satanic, evil forces, but there would come a 'Man' who would defeat those forces. That was fulfilled in Jesus.

God prophesied to Abraham that his descendants would be 400 years as slaves in Egypt. And so it came to pass.

God promised, hence prophesied, to Abraham that his descendants would be uncountably numerous and all the world would be blessed by one of them. The numberless Jews to be found world-wide and the coming of their Messiah, Jesus, testify to the fulfillment of that prophecy.

Jewish prophets are recorded as prophesying that the Jews in Israel would be conquered by the Babylonians and held in exile for 70 years. And so it came to pass.

The timing of the birth of Jesus was prophesied by Daniel and its location in Bethlehem by Micah. These prophecies were fulfilled in every detail.

The coming of the Jewish Messiah, His suffering, manner of death and resurrection, were all prophesied centuries before they were fulfilled.

Equally convincing are the prophesies of over 2000 years ago which are being fulfilled today: The return of the Jews to their own land; Israel the centre of world attention and Jerusalem no longer controlled by Gentiles.

As the Bible records accurately hundreds of prophecies centuries before the events prophesied happened, and those fulfillments are well attested, surely it can be trusted to record accurately the origins of the universe and people.

(4) Freedom of choice

Imagine the scene if, one day, on planet earth there was no human being. Then, on the following day, there appeared a physically adult man with fully developed mental abilities—able to think and speak a language.

If such a situation could be proved scientifically or demonstrated to be true, no one would be free to reject the clear evidence of the intervention of a supernatural, intelligent and powerful being who 'created' that man. Such a situation could not come about as a result solely of natural forces. It could not have evolved.

That such an event took place but is not verifiable scientifically is evidence of the biblical truth that He has given men and women a *unique choice* and that choice includes the possibility of rejecting His existence. The 'hiddenness' of God in the Genesis record, the creation of 'man' as a mature adult, and of the universe in an apparently advanced state of development confirm the fundamental principle of 'freedom of choice'.

This situation is expanded in Chapter 9.

(5) The Bible in human experience

Although probably the least open to scientific verification, the most powerful support for the truth of the Bible lies in the experience of those who trust it. For over two thousand years men and women have been using the Bible to direct their lives and find in it a purpose for living, a power to face evil and a hope for life after human death. It is this experience of the God of the Bible which leads to the trust placed in what He has caused to be written to make that experience possible.

When God is big enough to fulfil His word in changing one's life, it is not difficult to trust His God-breathed word to be accurate about the origins of life.

Conclusions:

Confusion in the Christian's defence of the biblical record of creation against secular, humanist, atheistic evolution lies in

(a) the lack of definitions of terms and understanding of the respective environments in which they work, and

(b) the muddled interpretation of the biblical record by Christians.

Four pivotal events:

While the creation/evolution confusion is evident in many situations where science claims to be in contradiction to the biblical record, four are pivotal:

(a) The origin of the universe
Creationist:

In the beginning, God created the universe as a vast array of celestial bodies so organized that they gave the appearance of an historical beginning from zero.
Christian evolutionist:

God created an initial equivalent of a 'Big Bang' beginning and then, after millions of years of 'void and darkness' a planet in the universe became habitable for life-forms.

(b) The origin of all life-forms
Creationist: God created all life forms 'after their kinds',
that is, cross-fertilizing species.
Christian evolutionist: God had created the components
life-forms but life appeared spontaneously and evolved from
the simplest cells to the most complex.

(c) The origin of 'man—male and female'
Creationist: God created the first man as a mature intelligent adult, modelled on the nature of His creator, with the
appearance of growth from infancy to maturity,
Christian evolutionist: At some point an evolved 'homi-
nid'—intermediate between ape and man, evolved into
'man' into whom God 'breathed spiritual life', as illustrated
in the myth of Genesis 1.

(d) A universal flood
Creationist: About 1500 years after creation, God destroyed
all air-breathing life on the earth's surface with the excep-
tion of eight persons and some air-breathing life in a large
ship. Vast quantities of rain falling from a melting ice-
canopy plus massive earthquake and volcanic earth movements moulded the earth's surface very much as it is today.
Christian evolutionist: All geological formations were laid
down over millions of years of changing climate and volcanic action. There probably was a flood or many floods as
attested by the historical records of early civilizations.

In each case, there are two alternatives: Belief in either
the biblical account or the unsubstantiated theories of scientists.

Some of the creation/evolution confusion is caused by a
lack of definition of terms. For the Christian, much of the
confusion lies in alternative interpretations given to the plain
meaning of the biblical narrative, compromised by an un-
justified faith in the unsubstantiated claims of science.

Chapter 9

A Christian Creationist's God-scenario

A question which faced me, the author, many years ago was to play a significant role in my strong conviction of the truth of the creationist's case. As a Christian from the age of 11 and brought up in an evangelical, missionary environment, it was not difficult for me to accept that God created the world and the people in it whom He loved sufficiently to suffer greatly for them.

My firm Christian convictions were challenged in four very different circumstances: Four and a half years in the Royal Air Force in which I completed 49 operational missions in an anti-shipping Coastal Command squadron; four years studying for a science degree and Teacher's Diploma, seventeen years as a Christian missionary in Rwanda and Burundi, Africa, and fourteen years lecturing in mathematics and mathematics education in London University.

My problem was that I did not find it possible to fit all the different aspects of my Christian faith into a coherent structure within which there were, in my understanding of them, no contradictions.

The final resolution and its application to the various truths of the Christian faith are spelled out in *"The hidden key to the God-scenario."* [1]

The crux of my searching could be summed up in one question: As God is the creator of the universe and of intelligent people, why is He hidden from them in a visible or tangible way?

I refer to people as intelligent in the sense that they are able and want to ask questions, observe happenings and situations, and, by reasoning from their observations, come to conclusions which affect their lives.

Would it not have been more efficient of God to be here with us in a visible, tangible form to explain to us why He created us and what He expects of us? That would include an explanation of how and why He brought the universe, our environment, into being. Would not such a course of action have avoided all the creation/evolution, good and evil, pain and suffering, confusion that exists today?

An early conclusion in my reasoning was that, if the Creator-God had reasons for bringing people into being, those reasons must include the necessity for Him to be hidden from them.

A particular aspect of what I understand to be the biblical answer to my question applies to the creationist/evolutionist confusion. This confusion is not an accident or the consequence of a weakness in God's communication to people of what He wants them to know. It is part of His strategy in achieving His purposes. The hiddenness of God is a very important factor in the coherent scenario that the Bible presents.

---

[1] H H Osborn *The hidden key to the God-scenario* Apologia

The explanation begins with the question: Why does anyone hide from anyone else? For fun, as in the game of hide-and-seek, to attack unseen the unsuspecting, to defend from attack or ... *to observe behaviour when the observer is not seen to be there*?

To somersault a considerable amount of reasoning, the only reasonable answer is that God is hidden in the universe, in the Bible and in human history so that each person can make a *unique choice* without the certainty that He exists. His known presence would limit freedom of choice.

Illustration

Imagine that you are an explorer in a part of the world which, as far as you know, has never been reached before by anyone. You come to a wide river and, to your astonishment, you see on either side of it, the remains of the two ends of what appears to have been a bridge across the river.

You make a boat and cross the river and note, again to your amazement, that the remains of both ends are very similar and bear the marks of the same builder. Surely there must have been, at some time in the past, a complete bridge across the river, constructed by the same engineer! Further investigation indicates that the width and depth of the fast-flowing river makes the construction of such a bridge an impossibility.

As an explorer, what would you make of that?

There are only two possibilities: either:

(i) the conditions were at some time in the past different from those at present and were such as to make the construction of a bridge possible, or

(ii) the engineer who built the two ends wanted people to believe that there was once a bridge across the river although there had never been such a construction and it would have been, in any case, impossible.

Most explorers would probably come to the first conclusion. It would appear to be the most reasonable.

The second explanation would appear to make the bridge builder a deceiver. He wanted to make people believe something which was not true! Only if there was an honest, valid, logical reason for building the two ends to be similar could the appearance of such an impossible situation be considered credible.

Take this a step further. You are an exploring biologist and you compare the biological structure of 'man' and that of apes. The genomes of both are very similar. In fact, the two are so much alike that you reason that, like the two ends of a bridge just described, there must have been a link between them—like a structure to link the two ends of the bridge.

You call that link an 'evolution' from one to the other.

When you come to study the process of such an evolution, it becomes increasingly clear that it is an impossibility. It is a good idea, but it has no basis in fact. The differences between the most human-like apes and any human being are so great that they could not possibly have been produced by many small modifications of their genetic codes. Furthermore, there is no example elsewhere in the living world of such a transition between 'kinds' of which the process has been fully explained or demonstrated to have happened. Fossil records are incomplete. No one has any idea how, except by chance mutations, such an evolution could have taken place. The chances of such a process having taken place between any two 'kinds' of life are very small. Then multiply that by the millions of different 'kinds' which exist. This places such evolutionary processes in the category of miracles! And miracles require a supernatural intervention. A 'bridge' between the two is, scientifically, impossible. At least, no one has yet achieved it.

The conclusion must be that God created 'man' and apes like the two ends of the bridge in the above illustration in order to make two explanations plausible:

(i) Some people, who do not want to believe in a supernatural intervention, will be convinced that the link between the two is a naturally occurring *evolution*, despite the lack of evidence to that effect. There is no need for God.

(ii) Other people, who want to believe in God, will be convinced that both 'man' and 'apes' were *created* two separate and distinct 'kinds'. There is no bridge between the two, as God has made quite clear in His record.

Both these conclusions are intelligent deductions from given evidence; neither is provable by scientific means. The difference between them is the *belief* that, in the first case, there is no supernatural intervention needed to explain the universe and the life-forms in it, and, in the second case, the *belief*, that a supernatural intervention is inescapable.

Because the second explanation presents God as having created 'man' as a fully mature adult human being and the universe as appearing to have prior existence, the accusation is made that God is a deceiver. Such an accusation would be true if it were not for a most important fact. In the biblical record, it is stated clearly and unambiguously that God created the universe and all life-forms in six days.

When medical researchers produce a placebo—and inert substance, to appear exactly like an active substance and use it in a controlled trial they surely cannot be accused of deception. The 'hiddenness' of the inert/active substances allows reactions to be tested which would not be possible if there were no placebo.

God created this universe and hid Himself in it for a specific purpose which He has made abundantly clear. It is the theory that the universe and people evolved without any supernatural intervention which is the 'placebo'.

Christian evolutionists are prepared to believe the Bible when it records that Jesus was born of a virgin, that He healed leprosy sufferers, that He fed 5000 men from five loaves and two fishes, that He cast out evil spirits from the demon-possessed, that in His death He paid the penalty for the sins of the world, that He rose from the dead and that He is coming again to judge the world ...

But they are not prepared to believe the record from the same Bible that God created the universe to appear in an advanced state of development, that He created a man as a fully mature adult, and that He covered the earth with a great flood to give the earth an appearance of a great age.

That the record of the origins of the universe and of people could have been worded such that the two different views could be held by intelligent people is surely a tribute to the God-breathed character of the Bible and of His hiddenness from people in order to offer them a completely free *unique choice*.

The unique choice

The solution to this apparently confusing enigma is in the Bible and it is simple: God created the universe and the people in it for a particular reason. He was going to give people an extremely important *unique choice* which would affect their lives now and after their physical death for ever. For that choice to be perfectly free and for which they would be individually responsible, they had to live in an environment where evidence for God would be there, but His existence would not be inescapable. Their *choice* would be an entirely personal one which required their acceptance or rejection of Him as God.

To grasp the nature and context of this *choice*, it is necessary to understand what God has revealed about it. No human being could have thought it out alone.

An early source of confusion arises here. Christians are often very confused as to how they should understand God. Most appear not to think it through. Theologians have not helped by presenting numerous ideas of the so-called mystery of the Trinity.

A simple reading of the Bible removes the confusion. God is three extremely powerful and intelligent Beings. Each is, by nature, God (adjective). The three together are God (noun). They are not three 'Gods'.

The three God-persons are bound together to form a kind of 'Family of God' by bonds of *light*—total openness and *love*—total commitment to each other.

The three God-Persons wanted to increase their family to include people, like themselves, who would not be 'Gods', but would want to share in their life of oneness held together by *light* and *love*.

God could create angels who would obey Him in every way, but He could not create beings who, of their own free will, with the knowledge of what it was like to be out His family, freely chose to be in that family.

To choose to be in the 'family of God' one had first to be *out* of that family. The Bible tells the story of how that situation was brought about.

Before the creation of the universe, God created spirit beings called 'angels'. They were given certain liberty and some of them rebelled against God, led by their leader, Satan. They were expelled from the 'family of God' to form the 'family of Satan'. There were then *two* families.

God created the universe and, in it, He created the first man and woman with whom He was in a perfect relationship, called a 'life' relationship in the 'family of God'. He then gave them a choice between what He wanted them to do and what they wanted to do. They chose the latter and were expelled from the 'family of God'. to join the 'family

of Satan'. The scene was then set for the possibility for
people to make a *unique choice* between staying on for ever
in the 'family of Satan' in which there are born, or of quit-
ting that family and being 'born again' into the 'family of
God'. All the descendants of Adam and Eve are born into
the 'family of Satan' and remain there unless something
happens to free them.

God so loved the people He had created that, even before they rebelled against Him, He had worked out the way
in which every man and woman who was born in the 'family of Satan' could quit that family and join the 'family of
God' on His conditions.

The Bible is the record of how God has made it possible
for men and women to experience both the consequences
of life, in the 'family of God' and in the 'family of Satan'
and then to make their free *unique choice* either to stay in
the family of Satan' or quit that family and be 'born again'
into God's family, with neither God nor Satan visible.

There was one further step in God's programme. As soon
as a person is conscious as a child, he or she acts according
to their own wishes, not God's. No one can do something
which is wrong in God's sight and then go back in time and
not do it. The wrongs, or sins committed are an impossible
barrier to joining the 'family of God'. God was prepared
for that situation. One of the God-Persons, Jesus Christ,
became a 'Man', a human God-Person.

As such He suffered in Himself the spiritual consequences of the eternal separation from 'God the Father' of
all the sins that people have committed and which keep
them from being in the 'family of God'.

The barrier to people born in the 'family of Satan' from
being 'born again' into God's family was potentially removed. The barrier is fully removed when a person re-
pents of their sin and trusts in what Jesus has done for them.

In order to maintain His hiddenness, God has made His every intervention in the world such that those who believe in Him see that it is God who has acted. For those who do not believe that He exists, He has provided alternative explanations which, for them, are equally convincing.

Seen in this context, the evidence for believing in the theory of evolution is God's alternative for believing in the creation record. The Bible makes it clear that He created the universe with planet earth in it. He created man—male and female as human models of Himself so that He could offer them a place in His family. 'Man', on planet earth, is the centre of the universe. Man—male and female, are the reason for its existence.

The atheist sees human beings as specks of dust in a vast universe whose only significant value is to perpetuate life. Otherwise, life is meaningless. Once their life-producing function is completed people decompose into the material compounds from which they emerged.

The creationist understands from the Bible that every man and woman is of such great value to their Creator, that He has gone to great lengths to enable them to live for ever in His family. However, membership of that family is only available to those who respond to His love for them as demonstrated in the events revealed in the Bible record. There can be no greater future for anyone.

The God-scenario presented by the creationist fits all the facts. To make the *unique choice* which God offers every man and woman, He has put them in an environment in which they can observe what life is like when lived according to one's self-centred interests, and what it is like when it is lived according to God's revealed plan. In that environment both God and Satan are hidden in a visible or tangible way, in order to make a person's choice absolutely free and for which each person is entirely responsible.

Conclusions

For those who do not want to recognize that they are
created humans beings with a responsibility to their creator, the 'theory of evolution', albeit unproved, is an ideal
alternative. Despite the fact that the world provides ample
evidence of the effects of self-centred behaviour, they avoid
the biblical fact that they will one day face their Creator
and give an account of the life they have lived on earth.
They can ignore their Creator's judgement that they will be
punished for all the pain and suffering to others they have
caused, and they will finally live in an environment—hell,
where there will be no God, hence no love or joy, and where
they will be able to satisfy to the full their self-centred wishes
without hurting anyone else.

For those who have learned from the Bible of God's
love for them, who have seen the pain and suffering that
evil produces; who have experienced in some Christian fel-
lowships the love and light that is in the 'family of God';
who have repented of their sin and rejected the 'family of
Satan'; who have trusted in what Jesus did in suffering, in
their place, the spiritual consequences of their sin and have
known God's forgiveness; who have made the *unique choice*
of asking God to forgive them and give them 'new birth'
into His family ...

For such, life is full of meaning, there is a God-planned
purpose for the lives of everyone, a freedom from the guilt
and final penalty for sins committed and an eternity in the
'family of God' where there will be only light and love.

God is hidden in the universe for a very wonderful purpose: Jesus said, *"For judgment I have come into this world,
so that the blind will see and those who see will become
blind."* [1]

God is hidden so that each person is free to choose: God
or no-God, creation or evolution, life or death.

[1] John 9:39

Chapter 10

Epilogue

Confusion is, perhaps, a necessary precursor of clarity. When, however, confusion is not recognized as such, there is little hope of clarity.

In the foregoing, two areas of confusion have been identified: in the creation/evolution dialogue and in the Christian creationist/Christian evolutionist relationship. In both situations, the definition of terms, the meanings attributed to them and the faith exercised in accepting what they mean, have been central. Partly, perhaps, due to this confusion, creationists have been the objects of false accusations. These are a form of persecution, so the advice of the Apostle Peter is appropriate:

"Who is going to harm you if you are eager to do good? But even if you should suffer for what is right, you are blessed. Do not fear what they fear; do not be frightened. But in your hearts set apart Christ as Lord. Always be prepared to give an answer to everyone who asks you to give the reason for the hope that you have. But do this with gentleness and respect," [1]

[1] 1 Peter 3:13

Here is the heart of the creationist's defence of biblical truth: The experiential—*"in your hearts set apart Christ as Lord"*, the intellectual—*"Always be prepared to give an answer to everyone who asks you to give the reason for the hope that you have,"* and the practical—*"do this with gentleness and respect."* This is an essential combination for effective communication and convincing defence of the faith..

Furthermore, for the Christian, the Apostle Paul's insistence is fundamental, that

"you must no longer live as the Gentiles do, in the futility of their thinking. They are darkened in their understanding and separated from the life of God because of the ignorance that is in them due to the hardening of their hearts." [1]

Paul recognized that, in his day as today, *"some people are throwing you into confusion and are trying to pervert the gospel of Christ."* [2]

In the past it has been possible in the UK for people to hold differing views while not enforcing those views on others or influencing their lives because of them. An important new factor has emerged which has changed this situation. The secular humanist promotion of the theory of evolution is so aggressive in this age that few can escape the much publicized claim that science has removed religion from the modern rational mind. For them, the only alternative to the evolution theory is blind faith in something which does not exist and for which there is no evidence. Secular atheists insist that not only is the evolutionary theory a true explanation for the appearance of life on this planet, but it *excludes* all other explanations. The consequences of this aggressive stance go beyond the academic debate, the scientific promotion of honest investigation of all phenomena of whatever form and the free expression of views in public places and institutions.

[1] Ephesians 4:17-20   [2] Galations 1:7

The trend is for the 'creationist' explanation of the origin of the universe and of life-forms on it, or any other possibilities, other than 'evolution' to be *prohibited* in all education. Even investigation into the possibility of Intelligent Design is to be *forbidden*. The moral foundations laid down by the Bible, are to be *rejected* except for those which are justified by social conditions. Where religion, which provides an alternative to 'evolution', opposes this view, *its practice and promotion must be controlled* to limit its effects.

This antagonism to biblical truth reintroduces a factor mentioned in Chapter 9 which atheism cannot accept as it does not accept the fact of 'God', that is, the fact of 'Satan', the adversary of God. A-theism is also a-satanism.

According to the Apostle Paul, *"The god of this age has blinded the minds of unbelievers, so that they cannot see the light of the gospel of the glory of Christ, who is the image of God."* [1]

The Christian recognizes that the hostility of the secular humanist evolutionist is not derived only from purely academic or intellectual sources, but is driven by supernatural evil forces.

The Bible is clear about the impact that observing the universe should have on every man and woman:

"The wrath of God is being revealed from heaven against all the godlessness and wickedness of men who suppress the truth by their wickedness, since what may be known about God is plain to them, because God has made it plain to them. For since the creation of the world God's invisible qualities—his eternal power and divine nature—have been clearly seen, being understood from what has been made, so that men are without excuse. For although they knew God, they neither glorified him as God nor gave thanks to him, but their thinking became futile and their foolish hearts

[1] 2 Corinthians 4:4

*were darkened. Although they claimed to be wise, they be-
came fools and exchanged the glory of the immortal God
for images made to look like mortal man and birds and
animals and reptiles. ... They exchanged the truth of God
for a lie, and worshipped and served created things rather
than the Creator—who is for ever praised. Amen."* [1]

The Bible is also clear about its message to the world:

*"The God who made the world and everything in it is
the Lord of heaven and earth and does not live in temples
built by hands. From one man he made every nation of
men, that they should inhabit the whole earth; and he determined the times set for them and the exact places where
they should live. God did this so that men would seek him
and perhaps reach out for him and find him, though he is
not far from each one of us. ... In the past God overlooked
such ignorance, but now he commands all people every-
where to repent. For he has set a day when he will judge
the world with justice by the man he has appointed. He has
given proof of this to all men by raising him from the dead."* [2]

In opposing the 'theory of evolution' the Christian creationist is not simply defending a different point of view of
concern to those interested in such matters. He is defending the communication of the Creator-God to every person
as recorded in the Bible.

Given the intelligence and power of God, as seen in the
universe, it diminishes His authority to twist the 'God-
breathed' word to mean anything other than it is clearly
and plainly intended to mean. And it undermines the power
of the Good News of Jesus Christ to achieve God's pri-
mary purpose—to 'save' people from their destiny, inherited from the historical Adam, to live with the God-Persons
in a recreated universe—'the new heavens and the new
earth',[3] inherited from the historical and ever-living Jesus.

[1] Romans 1:18-25   [2] Acts 17:24-31   [3] Revelation 21:1 ff